START AND RUN

YOUR OWN COFFEE SHOP AND LUNCH BAR

START AND RUN

YOUR OWN COFFEE SHOP AND LUNCH BAR

Heather Lyon

howtobooks / **smallbusinessstart-ups**

Published by How To Books Ltd
Spring Hill House, Spring Hill Road
Begbroke, Oxford OX5 1RX United Kingdom
Tel: (01865) 375794
Fax: (01865) 379162
info@howtobooks.co.uk
www.howtobooks.co.uk

British Library Cataloguing in Publication Data
A catalogue record of this book is available from the British Library

ISBN: 978-1-84528-283-7

Produced for How To Books by
Deer Park Productions, Tavistock, Devon
Designed and typeset by Mousemat Design Ltd
Printed and bound by Cromwell Press, Trowbridge, Wiltshire

NOTE: The material contained in this book is set out in good faith for general guidance and no liability can be accepted for loss or expense incurred as a result of relying in particular circumstances on statements made in the book. Laws and regulations are complex and liable to change, and readers should check the current position with relevant authorities before making personal arrangements.

This book is dedicated to Robert Pirrie, my late partner,
who initially encouraged me to write this book.

CONTENTS

ACKNOWLEDGEMENTS

I would like to thank Nikki Read at How to Books for her expertise, encouragement and all her editorial contributions during the initial stages of the book.

My heartfelt thanks to Gordon and Dorothy Swan for all their time, support, encouragement and knowledgeable help over the last few months.

My special thanks to Adrian and Julie Hodge for their time, support and outstanding contributions to this book.

My sincere thanks to Paul Wigley and Mark Gregory for their time and useful contributions.

Finally, I would like to thank my local Environmental Health Department for their expertise and very helpful contribution.

PREFACE

So you want to open and run your own coffee shop!

Many people dream about starting their own business and once you have done it you won't want to go back to working for anyone else. You can get started in business with a relatively small investment and realize a good profit if you make a success of your enterprise.

Starting and running your own coffee shop is an exciting and satisfying challenge and can give you a good income, providing you are prepared to invest a lot of time and energy into making it successful.

However, to have a good idea is one thing; being able to turn your idea into a business is quite another. Before you decide to go into business it is essential that you consider very carefully the advantages and disadvantages of owning your own business.

Advantages

- □ Pride in owning and running your own coffee shop.

- □ Potential to earn more than you would if you were employed.

- □ Flexible working hours.

- □ You make all the decisions regarding your business.

Disadvantages

- □ You will have a high level of responsibility.

- □ You won't have a regular fixed income.

- □ You will probably have to work long hours.

- □ You have the responsibility of making difficult decisions.

Now ask yourself a few questions before you make any decisions.

- □ Do you like being in charge?

- □ Can you delegate?

- □ Can you cope with stress?

- □ Are you customer friendly?

☐ Can you be positive through the bad times as well as the good times?

☐ Are your family supportive about you starting your own coffee shop?

☐ Does the prospect of financial insecurity motivate rather than scare you?

☐ Are you prepared for hard work and long hours?

☐ Are you prepared to work weekends and public holidays?

☐ Are you able to sacrifice some things, such as holidays, and to cut back financially until you get your coffee shop established?

☐ Are you prepared to learn new skills?

☐ Do you have self-motivation, determination and stamina?

☐ Are you in good health?

☐ Do you believe in yourself?

These questions are not meant to put you off opening your coffee shop but to make you think about the skills you require. If you are able to answer yes to all the questions, and you are still passionate about opening your own coffee shop, you should learn as much as you can about this business; do your research and get to know your market.

There are many reasons why businesses fail within a few years: perhaps because there has not been enough effort put into understanding the importance of getting the best location possible; perhaps not enough research has been done, or not enough capital raised to get started; perhaps the business plan was not a good one; maybe failure is down to lack of organisation and management skills, or not employing the right staff, or simply being unable to be that bit better than your competition.

The most important thing you should do when starting your business is to make sure you are well prepared. This comprehensive book will give you all the information and advice you will ever need to help you set up and run your own coffee shop. In it I have given you my advice and experience, along with expert tips, popular recipes and crucial data to help you make the most of your coffee shop. The practical information contained in this book, together with the commitment and passion you have for your coffee shop, will ensure that your chances of success are high.

1
GETTING STARTED

Planning Your Business

One of the first decisions you have to make, and possibly one of the most difficult, is: Are you going into business alone or with a partner or partners?

GOING INTO BUSINESS WITH FRIENDS OR FAMILY

A partnership is defined as an association of two or more people to carry on a business with a view to making a profit.

You have probably thought of going into business with a friend or your spouse. However, no matter how well you get on with your friend or spouse, there will always be disagreements when starting and running a business. Unless you can agree on most things, in my view, you should keep your friendship separate from your business. Spouses on the other hand are used to making joint decisions and working through financial problems, so going into business together could work out.

If, however, you do want to go into business with a friend I would suggest that you consult a solicitor who is experienced in commercial law and ask him or her to draw up a partnership agreement. It will seem a nuisance at the start but it could save a lot of unforeseeable problems in the future. If business partnerships are formed without any forethought they are more than likely to be doomed to failure.

Informal agreements can fall apart whereas a partnership agreement outlines the contribution that each partner will put into the business and it defines the roles of the partners.

> *I know of a business that collapsed because when two friends decided to start a business together they thought that their friendship was strong enough to stand up to any difficulties which they would encounter in their partnership. One of the partners continually took time off to attend to family commitments and left the other partner to cope with running the business. They had not entered into a partnership agreement and unfortunately when their business collapsed so did their friendship. I feel that it is essential to get good legal advice if you are considering entering into any type of partnership.*

If you do decide to go into partnership with someone, give it a lot of thought and choose the person very carefully. If you don't trust that person, don't even consider starting a business with him or her.

SOME OF THE ADVANTAGES OF HAVING A PARTNER

☐ You will be working with someone you can trust and who you know will not let you down.

☐ You will be able to cover each other's holidays or time off for family events etc.

☐ You share the risk of starting a new business.

☐ At the outset you will both be able to contribute an equal share of money to start up the business. This should enable you to spend more money on your premises and on fitting out your coffee shop.

☐ You have a combination of ideas and the experience of two or more people to help set up and run your coffee shop. Everyone has different skills and talents which they bring to a business and this is beneficial.

☐ You share the responsibility for business debts.

☐ Shared decision-making can be a good thing as it increases your confidence in making the right choices.

SOME OF THE DISADVANTAGES OF HAVING A PARTNER

☐ One partner may not be able to work such long hours as the other due to family commitments and this may cause ill feeling and lead to arguments.

☐ The profits will have to be shared and you will have to agree with your partner when they can be taken out of the business and what they are going to be used for. What percentage of the profit is going to be put back into the business to improve it, for example, redecorating or buying new equipment, or will the profit just be shared equally for the partners to spend as they wish?

☐ Decision-making has to be shared as you will have to obtain the approval of your partner. You can't just decide to sell the business or close it for two or three weeks while you go on holiday without your partner's agreement.

☐ If the business fails it is very likely that it will put a tremendous strain on the relationship with your friend and you will have to be prepared to lose that friendship.

☐ If one partner dies, or wants to terminate the partnership, the other partner will have to find the capital to take over the business as sole owner or proprietor.

If you are absolutely certain that you want to go into business with your partner or spouse and you both have the same goals and aspirations, then discuss it fully. I would recommend that you put an informal partnership agreement together which will define issues like your areas of responsibility and share of profits before you go into business.

Thinking about your business agreement

You may wish to consider the following issues when making a business agreement with your spouse or civil partner:

☐ What will happen if one of you has to take maternity leave or has to take a long period off work due to illness?

☐ How do you want the business and property to be shared?

☐ Are you agreed on what each partner will be able to draw as a salary, and how the profits will be distributed?

☐ Are you agreed on what hours each partner will work?

☐ Are you agreed on how you will divide your responsibilities? For instance, one of you may have management skills and the other may have customer skills, so stick to what you do best.

> *When I was young and inexperienced I helped my husband in his retail business but sometimes he would go off to play golf and I was left to work in the shop and watch the children at the same time. If we had initially discussed and agreed on the terms of working in the business, these problems might not have arisen.*

In conclusion, whatever type of partnership you enter into, make sure it is an equal partnership and that the work is divided equally. However, you should be flexible and be prepared to give and take in certain circumstances if one of you requires extra time off for something special.

 You can form a limited liability partnership which is similar to a normal partnership but also reduces personal responsibility for debt. For more information on this go into the website www.companieshouse.gov.uk

Choosing a location

The location of your coffee shop can be a major contribution to its success or failure. Choosing the most suitable location may therefore be your single most important decision. It requires a great deal of thought and planning. Don't just decide to rent or buy a shop because it is inexpensive; if you choose the wrong location you could be setting yourself up to fail. A poor location is one of the major causes of failure for a business whereas a good location is sometimes all it takes to make your business thrive.

The best way to choose a location for your coffee shop is by doing research. This allows you to build up a picture of potential areas and also allows you to look at the pros and cons of each area so that you can choose a location that gives your business the most advantage.

You should consider the following points before making your decision on a location.

☐ What competition is there in the area?

☐ Is there adequate parking?

☐ How close is it to your customer base?

☐ Is there a steady flow of foot traffic which will guarantee walk-in customers?

☐ What image do you want your coffee shop to project?

It cannot be stressed enough that the location of your enterprise is of paramount importance. What follows are a few comments on the principal categories of coffee shop location.

A SHOP ON THE MAIN STREET

The most desirable location for a coffee shop, in my opinion, would be situated on a main shopping street which has a steady flow of foot traffic as most of your business will come from people walking past. However, this is not absolutely necessary and if you can rent space in a large retail outlet you can make it just as successful.

 You could choose a shop in a popular busy area of town which may be a student area or consist of other shops, businesses and offices. You would then benefit from a stable customer base and would have constant passing foot traffic.

 Good visibility and easy access are beneficial because the more people who know that your coffee shop exists, the better. There is no use in having the most fantastic coffee shop up a lane or above another shop or business because that is putting you at an immediate disadvantage.

The benefit of opening a coffee shop on a prime site in a busy town is, if you can afford it, huge. You just have to concentrate on making your coffee shop better than the competition and somewhere that people will want to return to again and again.

The downside of opening a coffee shop in a prime area is the high price you will have to pay for rent and rates. You will have to make enough money to cover these expenses before you make any profit.

Buying or renting an established business

You may decide to purchase or rent an already established coffee shop situated in a prime position. The benefit of this is that you will be able to see what the turnover of the business is from their prepared accounts and whether you think you can improve on that turnover. You will also have the benefit of an existing customer base that you can build on so that you do not have to start from scratch.

In addition, it may be easier to get finance by producing a business plan, together with the prepared accounts, to show the bank what profit the previous owner made and how you intend to improve it.

An already established coffee shop should include all fittings and fixtures and it should already have a kitchen fitted out. If the fittings and fixtures are in quite good condition and you think that you can make do until you can afford to change them, it is worthwhile having them included in the sale or lease agreement. This will save a lot of expense initially if you are working on a tight budget and you should not need to replace any large items until you make enough profit to do so. However, you may want to invest in a few up-to-date items such as a good commercial microwave, a toasted sandwich machine, a contact grill for making paninis and a good commercial dishwasher (a godsend) if a dishwasher is not already installed. On the other hand, if the equipment is in poor condition it would be worth asking the landlord or owner to have them removed. You will then have a blank canvas to design your own kitchen.

You will probably want to redecorate the coffee shop to your taste and perhaps add a few items such as bright, pretty tablecloths, blinds or fashionable curtains. If the flooring is shabby you could put down a hard-wearing, easy-to-clean type of flooring or carpet tiles which you can replace if someone stains the tile and the stain can't be removed. Carpet tiles can be vacuumed at night and shampooed if required. Whatever you choose, try to make your coffee shop warm and inviting.

A SHOP WITHIN A RETAIL STORE

Another option is to open your coffee shop in a retail unit like B&Q, Homebase, a garden centre, a bookshop or somewhere similar. Anywhere that you think there is a need for a coffee shop and there is a good customer base already.

The benefit is that there is an established customer base coming into the shop who will potentially visit your coffee shop if you make it attractive to them. Many of the retail shop's customers would probably be happy to be able to sit down and enjoy a hot drink and something to eat while shopping. If you offer a good service with good food and beverages at a reasonable price they will return and also tell their friends about it. Your business will soon be booming and it will also help to increase the business of the retailer.

Our coffee shop is situated in a large retail unit in a small town. It is very busy, especially at weekends and during the school holidays.

The only downside that I can think of is that if the retail store is open seven days a week you will probably have to open your coffee shop every day.

Look around your area and if there are any large, busy retail units that you think would be suitable, approach the owners.

> *I was in Cambridge recently and visited a retail park just outside the town. Although there were some large retail units situated there, not one had a coffee shop where we could get something to eat and drink. We were so desperate for a drink and a snack that we went to a supermarket on the site and bought a sandwich and a cold drink and returned to sit in the car to eat and drink them. Here was an ideal opportunity for someone to open a really good business within one of these large retail units. A healthy profit could be made if you served good food at a reasonable price. Alternatively, you could set up a coffee and sandwich stall in a retail site.*

 If you decide on renting space in an already established retail unit make sure you get a lease and agree a reasonable rent for the area you are intending to use.

How to negotiate space in a retail shop

Prepare a well-thought-out, well-written and nicely presented business proposal. Make sure your proposal sounds attractive to the retailer and is open-ended enough to allow you room to negotiate. Make a list with details of ways in which you think your coffee shop would benefit their business. Below is an example of what your list could include.

☐ Your coffee shop will increase customer volume and potential profit for the retail store. There is potential for your customers to look around the retail store and purchase something before or after visiting your shop.

☐ You could offer a discount to the staff in the retail store. This would be a benefit to the retailer as they would be able to offer this perk when employing staff, especially if there is no place to purchase food in the vicinity of the store.

☐ Produce a sample menu which will let the retailer know what type of food and drinks you are intending to serve.

☐ Draw a plan (or get your architect to sketch one for you) of what you intend the coffee shop to look like so that the retailer will have some idea of what type of shop it will be.

☐ Your shop will enhance the retail store.

☐ If you advertise your coffee shop in the newspaper or on the local radio station, potentially it could bring new customers to the retail store. You could ask the local newspaper to write a feature, with photographs, on the opening of your coffee shop, to let the public know where you are and what you intend to offer them.

If it is agreed that you can rent a portion of the retail store, enquire if the store would be prepared to set up the coffee shop and lease it to you. If they only want to rent you the space, you would have to purchase all the equipment and set up the coffee shop yourself. However, if you are purchasing all the equipment yourself, then you may be able to negotiate the first few months rent free to allow you to get started.

 If your coffee shop is situated in a retail store it is a good idea to place a blackboard at the entrance of the store to advertise your business and make it obvious to customers that you exist.

A COFFEE STALL

Another option is to find a site to set up a coffee stall.

The benefit is that, if you find the right site, you can often make a lot of money from your business as you do not have the same overheads as the owner of a shop.

The downside is that it can be cold and if the weather is very bad it could affect your takings.

You can see coffee stalls situated in railway stations, shopping centres and markets all over the country.

Some coffee stalls in railway stations have tables and chairs situated around the stall. They serve coffees and teas and perhaps hot soup, rolls filled with bacon, sausage or egg and ready-made sandwiches for customers to take away or eat at one of the tables. They also tend to sell chocolate biscuits, muffins and sweets. Initially you would be able to run this type of business single-handed and if you build up a good business, you could then employ another member of staff.

Before embarking on setting up a coffee stall or kiosk you should check with your local Environmental Health Department to see what is legally required for this type of business.

A FRANCHISE

Some coffee shops and coffee stalls are franchised. The franchise company takes on much of the responsibility for decision-making. It grants you the right to sell its products.

The benefits are that the company may offer you a good site and give you start-up offers and good background information on running your shop, stall or kiosk. You benefit from the goodwill that the name and reputation of the franchise has already generated, and also from the support of the company in the selection of a location. Usually you will get free advertising and support during your initial set-up period.

The downside is that the company will want a reasonable share of your profit so you should weigh up the pros and cons of this type of set-up. The amount you will have to pay the franchisor for the benefits provided could be more than 10%. You will more than likely be restricted in what you are allowed to sell and you must adhere to the franchisor's standards. If you are considering taking out a franchise you should:

☐ learn as much as you can about the whole franchise process;

☐ find out what questions to ask the company with which you are thinking of taking out the franchise;

☐ if possible, take advice from other people who already have that franchise in order to determine the pros and cons.

If you do decide to take out a franchise make sure you get the promises made by the company written into the agreement.

Think very carefully about taking out a franchise because it is not easy to recover from choosing the wrong franchise company.

Check out the internet for more information about which companies will franchise on www.franchisedirect.co.uk

No matter where your coffee shop is situated, as long as you have done your homework and know that the chosen location has the potential to be busy, you are halfway there.

Offering a delivery service

Wherever you open your coffee shop you could offer a delivery service to staff in surrounding businesses. Staff working in local authority offices – for example, social services, housing departments, the police station and also local banks – are always pleased to try new places that offer good food at a reasonable price. Most of these office workers are too busy to spend time in their lunch break waiting for service in a coffee shop and would be delighted to have their order delivered to them.

If you do offer a delivery service, you will either have to deliver the orders yourself or employ someone to do this for you. You could do it yourself until you have an order service established and then if you think it will be profitable you could employ someone for a specific time, e.g. first orders 12.00 noon and last orders 2 p.m. If you employed someone you would also have to be prepared to allow them to use your car or to pay them mileage for the use of their own car.

Doing your research

You have some great ideas and you are eager to get started but first of all you have to test your market and this involves serious research.

Market research is essential; the success of your business may depend on it. You need to know who your competition is and you need to assess the customers who will support your business.

CHECKING OUT THE COMPETITION

Once you have identified the town, village or retail shop where you want to open your coffee shop, check out the surrounding area to see what competition, if any, you will have.

Study your potential competitors and think how you could make your coffee shop more appealing. What could you do to ensure that it stands out from the others?

Look at your competitors in terms of:

☐ location;

☐ quality;

☐ presentation;

☐ price;

☐ service;

☐ reputation;

☐ surroundings.

When you have done this, consider what they don't serve that you could.

Your competitors will be just as interested in you as you are in them and they won't wait around for you to get established. They will use various tactics to hang on to their business: for example, reducing their prices; introducing new items to their menu; aggressive marketing; refurbishing their shop.

Visit as many coffee shops as you can and take note of what they have to offer in terms of price, quality and presentation of coffee and cakes as well as décor and atmosphere. If you find a coffee shop that you would like to model your own on and it is not in the same location as where you are going to open your shop, ask the owner for some advice and tips.

I asked someone in another town for some advice and information and the coffee shop owner was only too pleased to help. He also gave me names and addresses of local suppliers which he had found had good products and were reliable. This information helped me enormously and saved me precious time going through the Yellow Pages.

If you find that there is competition, do make sure that particular area can support more than one coffee shop. Some competition is good for business as it makes you work harder to build up your enterprise and prevents you from becoming complacent. However, there is no point in going to all the expense of fitting out a new shop if there is not going to be enough business in the area to support an additional coffee shop. You will be setting yourself up to fail before you even get started.

 **Ask friends and family what they would expect from a coffee shop. Do they go to a specific place because they enjoy the coffee, the cakes or the atmosphere?   Your friends will be quite happy to give you their thoughts on what makes a good coffee shop.**

Ultimately, you will have to judge whether or not another coffee shop will succeed on the basis of your experience, information gathering and intuition.

> *I knew some people who did not research the market before opening a coffee shop and opened their shop in a small village. Although they were situated on the main street, there was no parking available.*
>
> *The owners refurbished their premises to a really high standard with good lighting and décor and the general atmosphere was appealing. However, their food was expensive and not particularly good and their customers did not return.*
>
> *The owners of the coffee shop thought that if they made a very good profit on everything they would be successful. They forgot that they had to work hard at getting customers through the door because of their location. They missed the opportunity of impressing their customers with good value for money. The quieter the business got the more depressed they became and if they had a particularly quiet day they would just close early. Their customers voted with their feet and didn't return.*
>
> *This particular coffee shop closed after being in business for a short time. The owners didn't do their research, they were in the wrong location, they didn't offer good food and coffee at a reasonable price and they didn't keep to their stated opening hours.*

Word of mouth is a great advert; if people are pleased with the food and coffee they are given they will tell their friends. However, this also works in reverse and if they don't like what they get, they will also tell their friends.

2
CHOOSING YOUR SHOP UNIT

Whether you choose to purchase or lease your own premises, it is a huge commitment so do make sure you consider all the pros and cons before making a decision.

Are you going to purchase or lease your premises?

It is difficult to say whether it is better to purchase a property or lease it. It depends on several factors, for example:

☐ whether you can afford to purchase the property you have chosen;

☐ whether the property you have chosen is available for purchase, or only for lease.

The reason that some properties are only available for lease is that many landlords prefer to retain their property because of the income it provides.

When you have completed your research and identified the property which you think is best for your coffee shop, discuss with your bank or building society exactly how much your monthly repayments will be. Add to this the costs of new equipment and setting up your business in order to get an accurate picture of the outlay ahead.

However, if purchase is not an option for you and you still think that this is the shop you really want then you should approach the owner to see if you can rent it for a period of time with the option to purchase it at a later date.

The most desirable agreement for you as you are starting a new business would be a two-year lease with the option to renew the lease at the end of the period and a guaranteed rent to be increased at a five-year period.

Alternatively, if the shop owner would agree to lease it to you for a period of one or two years with an option to purchase the property at the end of this period, this would allow you to see how much profit you can make before making a commitment to purchase the premises. Also you will be able to purchase it at market value without having to compete with other interested parties.

Purchasing your premises
ADVANTAGES OF PURCHASING

☐ Purchasing a property will give you an investment which, if it is in a good area, will increase in value. In the future, if you decide to retire you can sell the property and make a profit, or lease it out to someone else. This will give you a good income.

□ Your mortgage repayments could be less than the rental payments.

□ You can claim interest payments against your tax.

□ You won't have large rent increases.

DISADVANTAGES OF PURCHASING

□ You may have to put down a large deposit as you won't get a 100% mortgage.

□ You will be responsible for maintenance, fixtures and fittings and decoration.

 Do not purchase a property in a poor site because it is less expensive. You will always struggle to attract customers and if you decide to sell or lease the property you may find it difficult. You could be left with an empty shop and no income.

Leasing your premises

A lease is a legally binding contract between the landlord and the tenant and it sets out the terms, conditions and obligations of both parties in relation to the tenancy.

ADVANTAGES OF LEASING

□ Leasing a property allows you to set up your coffee shop with the smallest outlay.

□ Leasing allows you to spend more money on equipment and décor for your coffee shop.

DISADVANTAGES OF LEASING

□ You many be exposed to a large rent increase.

□ You will always have to get permission from your landlord to change anything in the shop.

Should you decide that you are going to lease, it is essential that you ask your solicitor to examine all the papers for you and discuss with you the implications of each clause before you sign. A lease is a very complex document.

NEGOTIATING THE TERMS OF YOUR LEASE

It is always worth negotiating the terms of the lease with the landlord because if it is unfavourable to you it could leave you with burdensome costs and liabilities. You may want to consider asking a solicitor who is familiar with leasing and purchasing commercial premises to negotiate for you. He or she will be able to draft your offer and may be able to negotiate a few months rent free or a few months at a reduced rent to allow you to set up and equip your coffee shop. Also, if there are any repairs to be carried out or any redecoration to be done, you could ask for a rent-free period or discount until these things are completed. If a rent-free period is agreed, ask your solicitor to insert a clause in the agreement stating what period of time you are allowed rent free.

If there are any items you want your landlord to leave in the premises, for example, fixtures and fittings, including kitchen equipment, or if you want your landlord to do any repairs before you take over the lease, your solicitor will insert a list of conditions in your offer to lease the premises. It is better to get these things agreed in writing before you take over the lease.

If you negotiate your lease you may be able to save yourself quite a lot of money. The rental price is not always the most important consideration for landlords. They may be more concerned with acquiring a good, reliable tenant than leasing the premises at a higher rent to a 'fly by night' tenant.

Your solicitor will be able to guide you in all aspects of the lease and will also be able to decipher the fine print on the lease that you may overlook.

You should always check with your local council on planning permission for change of use and for putting up a sign. Your solicitor should be able to do this for you.

☐ When taking out a lease on a shop, unless you are sure that you want a long lease, you may want to consider taking a short lease on the property with the option to renew it after a period of time.

☐ If possible, negotiate a cancellation clause which would safeguard you if you had to terminate your lease. You could agree a fee which would be payable to the landlords to allow you to terminate the lease.

I know someone who took out a long lease on the property they were interested in; unfortunately, when their circumstances changed, they were unable to sublet it. This was because the landlord had the right to vet each person interested in the property and if they didn't consider them suitable tenants, the sublet would fall through. If the landlord does not approve of the potential new tenant you will probably have to continue to pay rent until the lease is finished unless you have included a cancellation clause in the lease.

You never know when your circumstances could change or you find that your business is not doing as well as you expected, so it is better to be cautious and if possible opt for a shorter lease. If, after being in business for a while, you know that you want to continue to trade in your premises, you could approach your landlord and enquire if you could increase the term of the lease.

Finally, before making a decision on whether to purchase or lease premises for your coffee shop, decide what is the best available site that will give you the greatest opportunity to make the most of your business. Once you have done this, look at all the financial aspects of your chosen property and if you think you can afford it and make money, then go for it whether it is for lease or purchase.

3
GETTING ADVICE

Working with professional advisers

Professional advisers are experts in business matters and will be able to offer you guidance on many aspects of your business.

It is important to build up a good and trusting relationship with your professional advisers because you will probably be working with the same ones for many years. If you get on well with them, don't consider changing simply in order to save a few pounds – you might not get such good service with someone else.

SOLICITORS

No matter how well you get on with your solicitor, make sure you ask them for a written quote for the work they are going to do for you. Never allow your solicitor to start work before they have given you a written quote for their fees and outlays (registration fees, searches etc.). This applies not only to solicitors but also to any professionals you are planning to employ, for example, a surveyor, architect or accountant. You would never dream of having your house painted or a new kitchen or bathroom installed without knowing exactly how much it is going to cost you so always get a quotation from the professional firms you are going to employ before instructing them.

I was employed as a secretary with a firm of solicitors for approximately 10 years and I know that clients who asked for a written quote for fees before going ahead were charged less than those clients who did not request a written quote prior to commencing the work.

Finding the right solicitor

It is very important to find a good solicitor who has experience in dealing with small businesses and who specialises in the leasing and purchasing of commercial property.

If you already have a solicitor that you know and trust, you should make an appointment with them to discuss your ideas about purchasing or leasing premises to use as a coffee shop. If you have decided to go into business with a partner, ask your solicitor to draw up a partnership agreement for you.

If the solicitor you consult is experienced in litigation then they probably won't have any experience in commercial law and you could ask them to refer you to another partner in the firm who does have this experience or to another practice. Although solicitors do not like to turn away business, I have always found that they would rather refer you to someone with more experience in this particular field in the hope that you will come back to them in the future for another legal transaction. However, if you don't have a solicitor, you could ask friends to recommend someone who they think is good, or you can contact the Law Society who keep a register of solicitors in your area who are experienced in this type of work.

Before meeting your solicitor, take time to write down all the questions you want them to answer because it is easy to forget something important, especially if you are excited or nervous.

Your solicitor should be able to recommend other professionals, for example, a good accountant, architect and surveyor, and if you require finance they should also be able to help you with your loan proposal and business plan.

ACCOUNTANTS

A good accountant is essential when starting a business, especially if you have no previous experience in setting up your own business. Your accountant is employed by you to make sure that you pay as little tax as possible. He or she will be able to advise you exactly what expenses you can claim back against your tax and also give you advice on other business matters.

☐ Your accountant's firm may be able to deal with PAYE and National Insurance contributions for your staff if you do not want to do this yourself. Or, alternatively, they should be able to advise you on how to do it yourself.

☐ They will be able to tell you how to keep records and what expenses receipts they require in order to claim back against your tax return.

☐ They know what allowances you will be entitled to against your tax return.

☐ They will be able to register you for VAT and show you how to complete your VAT return.

Finding an accountant

Your solicitor may be able to refer you to an accountant that they know will deal with small businesses. Alternatively, you may be recommended one by friends or family. However, if you are still unable to find an accountant you can contact the Institute of Chartered Accountants and they should be able to give you details of local accountants.

Get into the habit of maintaining good records and keeping all your receipts because if your accountant has all the information required then they will be able to complete your tax return in a shorter time than if they have to keep contacting you for further information. Paperwork is an important part of your business and if your accountant can complete your return quickly it should cost you less.

Remember, you will have to use an accountant every year to complete your annual tax return unless you are able to do this yourself. Your accountant will be able to guide you on how to pay the least tax using all the allowances to which you are legitimately entitled. They will also be able to advise you about VAT registration, PAYE and National Insurance.

Again, do ask your accountant for a quote for the work to be carried out for you as this may also save you money in the long run. They may not be able to give you the exact cost of the work to be done but I don't see any reason why you cannot get a close estimate.

SURVEYORS

Surveyors offer impartial specialist advice on property issues.

Finding a surveyor

Your solicitor will instruct a surveyor to conduct a survey on any property you are planning to purchase. If by any chance you don't want to use the firm of surveyors recommended by your solicitor, you can contact the Royal Institute of Chartered Surveyors; their website is www.rics.org. You can search on that site for a suitable surveyor in your area. The RICS is the regulating body for chartered surveyors.

 **TIP** — Don't be tempted to ask for a walk-through valuation because it is cheaper. It is probably a false economy as it is a valuation only and does not go into detail about any essential repairs which have to be carried out. You want to know, for example, if there is any damp, woodworm, dry rot, wet rot, if the property requires rewiring or the building is subsiding. Always get an in-depth survey and not just a walk-through valuation.

If you are buying a property

The surveyor will give you the market value of the property and let you know what repairs are necessary. If they think the property is in need of a number of repairs and in poor condition, they may ask your lender to retain an amount of your loan equal to the cost of carrying out the repairs until they are completed, or if the property is in really bad condition, they could advise the lender not to lend any money on the property until all the work has been completed.

If you are borrowing money on the property you will be required to have a survey carried out by a surveyor who is approved by the bank or lending institution which is providing your loan. They will receive a copy of the survey, as will your solicitor. It is important to sit down with your solicitor and go through the survey report thoroughly because a bad survey report could be the deciding factor on whether or not you go ahead with the purchase.

If you are leasing a property

If you are leasing the property a surveyor could check out the building to see if it requires any major repairs. If so, you should ask the owner to carry out these before you take occupancy of the shop. The surveyor will also be able to give you an idea of the market rent for the premises you have decided to lease.

ARCHITECTS

An architect is best involved at the earliest planning stages and can manage your project until it is completed. They can advise and help you if you are planning to change the use of the property – for example, from a dress shop to a coffee shop – or if you want to carry out any alterations to the property. Remember, you will need permission from your local authority to carry out any major alterations to the premises and in these circumstances a good architect is worth their weight in gold.

Finding an architect

Personal recommendation is a good way to find an architect. However, if you don't know anyone who can recommend one, you can contact the Royal Institute of British Architects at www.architecture.com to help you choose the right architect for your project, whether it is large or small.

BANKS AND BUILDING SOCIETIES

Finance does not always need to be raised through a bank or building society. There are other ways; for example, you may be able to borrow money from friends and family or, as a last resort, you could remortgage your house. However, for many people, the bank or building society is the first port of call.

Getting the best deal

Shop around to find the best bank or building society to suit your needs. There is a lot of competition between them to attract new business. Find out whether you will be tied to the institution that is going to lend you money to start your business. If you do not need to get a loan for your business, or if you are not tied into a specific institution, you should check out interest rates and charges with a few banks and building societies and negotiate the rate of interest you will pay. Charges vary for such things as overdrafts, dishonoured cheques and supplying change, so get the best deal you can.

If the name of your business does not include your own name you must open an account under the business name. Cheques made payable to your company can then be paid into this account.

If you are borrowing from a bank you may find they have a pro forma business plan already set out. All you have to do then is to supply the information required. Do speak to the business manager to enquire if they have a pro forma business plan before going to the trouble of completing one yourself. (See pages 21 – 24 for details on drawing up a business plan.)

INSURANCE BROKERS

You should always plan for potential problems when opening your coffee shop and if possible insure against them.

Insurance brokers claim to be independent of any specific company, and state that they will try to find you the best insurance cover for the lowest premium. They are knowledgeable about different types of insurance policies and can advise you on the best one to suit your needs. Enquire if the broker has experience in insuring coffee shops, cafés and restaurants; if not, go to someone else who has this experience.

In any case, it is important that you obtain quotes from another two insurance brokers before making a decision about who you are going to take out your insurance policy with.

Again, personal recommendation is invaluable. If you have friends who run coffee shops or restaurants, ask them to recommend insurance companies, then approach these companies for quotes.

Understanding insurance

There are several types of insurance cover you must consider; basically, you need insurance to cover the building, contents and your liabilities. The main types are listed below.

GENERAL LIABILITY

☐ This covers you for negligence that results in injury to your customers and employees.

PRODUCT LIABILITY

☐ This covers you for problems that arise caused by any food or drink you serve on your premises. For example, you would be liable if a customer found a foreign object in anything you serve in your coffee shop. Customers will sue you for anything they can, so insure against this.

FIRE, THEFT, STORM, TEMPEST, MALICIOUS DAMAGE AND GLASS COVER INSURANCE
BUSINESS INTERRUPTION INSURANCE

☐ This covers lost income in the event that your business has to be interrupted. This could be because of flooding or damage to your property. The amount covered is based on your previous year's income for the same time of year, not on your figures for the busiest period of trade. The cover is to replace the lost income for the time you are unable to continue your business.

We had to wait several months before we received payment from the insurance company for a claim for flood damage and loss of earnings.

Insurance companies often send a loss adjuster to your premises to negotiate the amount of money that the company will agree to pay your business. This process can take quite a long time so, when you take out the policy, ask if you can get a policy that will give you payment weekly to cover your costs.

BUILDING AND CONTENTS INSURANCE

☐ This should cover the cost of replacing and repairing your buildings and contents so you must be sure to get a realistic quote and include extras for the cleaning up of the premises, removal of debris and any professional fees which might be incurred.

☐ Make a list of all the items you want covered and then get your quotes.

Finding help in your area

Government-supported agencies located throughout Britain offer information for people who are starting their own business. It is worth looking at the website which covers your own area to find out if you could benefit from the type of help they are offering. Information and support are available in the form of:

☐ start-up seminars;

☐ training courses;

☐ advice on financial management;

☐ sales and marketing advice;

☐ advice on helping existing businesses to grow;

☐ help and guidance in applying for a grant;

☐ access to database which contains information about grant and support schemes from central and local government;

☐ updates on relevant regulations.

Listed below are the contact details for the agencies.

ENGLAND

Business Link, tel.: 0845 600 9 006; website: www.businesslink.gov.uk

WALES

Business Eye, tel.: 08457 96 97 98; website: www.businesseye.org.uk

SCOTLAND

Small Business Gateway, tel.: 0845 609 6611; website: www.bgateway.com

HIGHLANDS AND ISLANDS ENTERPRISE

The Highlands and Islands have their own government-supported agency to assist and support new and existing businesses. The agency offers:

☐ business support services;

☐ training and learning programmes;

☐ information on business finance.

Tel.: 01463 234171; website: www.hie.co.uk

NORTHERN IRELAND

Invest North Ireland, tel.: 028 9023 9090; website: www.nibusinessinfo.co.uk

When do you need a licence?

You will have to obtain a licence to:

☐ sell alcohol;

☐ provide entertainment such as live music;

☐ play recorded music (contact the Performing Rights Society);

☐ sell food from a stall or van on the street.

To find out more information on licences you should contact your local authority.

Drawing up a business plan

Many people new to business often miss out the vital step of preparing a business plan when they are thinking about starting a business. It takes time and discipline to write an effective business plan but it is vital to think about your costs and how you will sustain the business.

When your bank manager or lender reads your business plan, they will know the name of your prospective business, what type of business it will be, the amount of loan you require and what the funds are to be used for.

Preparing a business plan has many benefits for you, too. It will help you to:

☐ think carefully about why you want to start your coffee shop;

☐ set your goals for the business;

☐ work out how much money you will need, from initially setting up and equipping the business to running it smoothly and profitably;

☐ look at the risks involved when starting a business;

☐ address the strengths and weaknesses of your proposed business;

☐ plan where you want to go in business and the best way to get there.

Your bank manager or finance manager will want to see that you have done your homework before lending you any money. Therefore, you will need a thorough, detailed business plan which should be specific about the use of the funds. You should support your request with estimates for work to be carried out and for purchasing equipment. Include a marketing strategy indicating who your prospective customers will be and how you will reach them. Your business plan should contain as much information as possible yet at the same time it must be concise.

YOUR BUSINESS PLAN SHOULD INCLUDE THE FOLLOWING:

A cover page which should include:

☐ the name of your business;

☐ business address;

☐ telephone number;

☐ date of preparation of the business plan;

☐ your own name.

A concise statement of the purpose and objectives of the business

☐ This part of the plan should give details of your proposed business.

☐ Outline the type of coffee shop you plan to open and stress the uniqueness of your shop and service; explain how you propose to attract your customers.

☐ State what you expect to accomplish in the future.

Full details of the management of your business

☐ If you are the sole owner of the business give your details, including any previous experience you have and any qualifications you may have.

☐ If you are going into business with a partner give their details, experience and qualifications also, and what skills they can bring to the business. Include a copy of the partnership agreement.

The location of your business

☐ If you have chosen a good location for your coffee shop, give your reason for choosing this location and emphasize its potential for attracting passing trade.

☐ If your coffee shop is situated beside well-known high street shops and businesses, state this fact.

☐ If there is good parking in the area you should include a diagram of the parking facilities.

☐ Include any drawings, plans and photographs you have of the proposed coffee shop and location. This will help the bank manager or lender to envisage what trade will be like.

What competition (if any) you will face

If you have competition, don't hide the fact but instead detail what you are proposing to offer your customers to make your coffee shop better and busier than any other coffee shops in the area. Compile an information sheet on your competitors, including:

☐ the names of other coffee shops;

☐ their location;

☐ their décor and atmosphere;

☐ the price and quality of their beverages and food;

☐ the service and staff attitude;

Then explain in detail how you plan to be better than the competition.

Your projected start-up costs

List what you think all your general expenses will be. These should include rates, rent (if you lease), electricity, gas, telephone bills, equipment, staff wages, together with loan repayments and advertising and any other expenses you can think of.

Some of these costs you will know, such as the rent, and if you don't know how much the rates will be you can contact your local council who will provide this information for you. You will be able to calculate staff wages by multiplying the total amount of hours worked by whatever hourly rate you are going to pay them. There is a minimum hourly rate set which you are legally bound to pay your employees.

The minimum wage applicable at the time of going to press is:

☐ age 16 – 17, £3.40 per hour;

☐ age 18 – 21, £4.60 per hour;

☐ age 22 and over, £5.20 per hour.

You can contact the National Minimum Wage Information Service for information on how much the current minimum wage is, or you can request their booklet, 'A Detailed Guide to the National Minimum Wage', by telephoning 0845 8450 360.

Electricity, gas and telephone expenses will be more difficult to calculate. If you already know someone who has a similar shop it would be worth asking them for an estimate of their utility costs.

If you are going to employ staff it is advisable to state at the beginning that no one should use the coffee shop telephone for personal calls. Instruct your staff that it should only be used for calls related to the business; for example, ordering supplies for the shop.

How much capital you require

This is again difficult to calculate but if you add together all your outgoings each week and allow some extra for unexpected expenditure you will have a rough idea. It will take a number of months before you are established and taking in enough money to make a profit. I recommend that you put aside a minimum of six months – if possible, one year's – expenses to help with the capital required to run the business.

Your projected turnover and profit/loss

Again this will be difficult to calculate but if you work out an average spend per customer and the number of customers you think will be in your shop per week you will be able to guess what turnover you will have.

If you have competition close by, you could sit in your car and count the number of customers that go in for coffee and multiply that by an average spend per head. This will give you an approximate figure for your projected turnover.

How you will deal with difficulties that may affect your business

You may unexpectedly have to take time off work – for example because of an accident or ill health. You should have plans in place to cover any such incidents. You could, for instance, train a good manager to run the coffee shop for you.

When you are preparing your business plan to present to the bank for the purpose of securing a loan, include a sketch of the layout of your proposed coffee shop, along with a sample menu with prices. It looks more professional if you laminate each page of your business plan and put them into a ring binder. This will keep all the pages in sequence and neatly together.

4
CREATING YOUR OWN COFFEE SHOP

You are aiming to create a coffee shop which is an attractive, congenial meeting place where friends and families can enjoy a warm welcome, excellent tea or coffee and pleasant company. Coffee shops are popular places to socialise over a drink and something eat. Age is no barrier when it comes to visiting a good coffee shop. Senior citizens visit them, mothers with young children meet their friends there, professionals dash in and out for a quick cappuccino and students sometimes study there while enjoying a coffee and a snack.

It is time to get your dream off the paper and turn it into reality.

Choosing a name

First impressions count, so it's important to choose the right name for your coffee shop. You should choose a name that reflects the type of image you want to project because that is what will draw in your customers and that is what they will initially remember about your coffee shop. You want your coffee shop to be one of the most important places in the community and it should be not only somewhere for people to gather and relax but also a place that they remember.

 When you are choosing a name, bear in mind that it will be easier for people to remember, pronounce and spell if it is made up of two syllables.

Your coffee shop's name will be on your external sign, your business cards, menus and perhaps on the napkins too, so make sure you choose a name that you really like because it will be expensive if you want to change it a few months later.

Listed below are a few things you should consider when choosing a name for your coffee shop.

- ☐ It should appeal to and attract potential customers;
- ☐ It should be easily remembered;
- ☐ It should be catchy;
- ☐ It should be unique and stand out from your competitors.

Ask friends and family to suggest ideas for names. Then write them all on a list and brainstorm them.

INVOLVING THE LOCAL COMMUNITY

One way of solving the problem – as well as generating useful publicity – is to approach your local newspaper and ask them to run a competition to choose the name for your coffee shop. You could announce the competition one week in a feature about you and your coffee shop, and the following week give the result, in another feature with photographs of you and the winner taken outside your coffee shop.

You would have to offer a prize to the winner; perhaps a free cup of coffee and a cake or scone for two, to be taken during a certain period of time, or a cash prize.

If you prefer, you could use your local radio station in the same way. Again this would give you free advertising (apart from the cost of the prize) for two weeks prior to opening. Whichever medium you decide to use, make sure you let people know where your coffee shop is situated, what you intend to offer your customers and when you intend to open.

If you do decide to have a competition to name your coffee shop, wait until you are just about to open so that the effect of advertising is not wasted.

Building an image
DESIGNING YOUR LOGO

Now that you have decided on the name of your coffee shop it is time to design a logo. A logo is a visual symbol which will serve as the signature piece for your business. Your coffee shop name and logo will help to establish a strong business identity. They can be put onto your letterheads, menus, napkins and business cards. Your logo will also be used when you advertise in your local newspaper and on any promotional material you give out, including flyers.

Give out as many business cards as you can to friends, customers and people you meet. You could also leave some in waiting rooms, for example, at train or bus stations and in doctors' and dentists' surgeries. This is an inexpensive way of advertising.

Creating the right atmosphere

You will have to take into consideration the kind of area your coffee shop is based in when you are thinking about the atmosphere you want to project. Are you in an area where your customers will predominately be shoppers or business people?

If you have competitors based in the same area you will also have to offer something quite different. The general atmosphere of your coffee shop should be appealing to your customers and to you. If you don't feel comfortable in the shop, your customers certainly won't.

The following are all important aspects to consider when you are creating a unique and appealing atmosphere for your coffee shop:

Lighting

Good lighting is essential but avoid harsh fluorescent lights which can cause headaches. Instead choose soft lighting which is bright enough to read by but gives a warm, cosy feel. Also good natural light from windows is great.

Music

Pleasant background music can enhance the atmosphere of a coffee shop. Invest in a good music system but don't play the music too loudly as customers will complain if they are unable to carry on a conversation. Ask your customers whether they prefer light music or no music at all. (Remember, if you decide to play recorded music you will have to obtain a licence from the Performing Rights Society.)

Furnishings

Whichever kind of atmosphere you are aiming for, your coffee shop must be a warm and inviting haven where people can relax in comfort. If it is in the style of an 'olde worlde' teashop, pretty tablecloths and matching curtains would help to create a traditional look, but make sure they also complement your colour scheme.

If your coffee shop has a more contemporary feel you might prefer modern blinds and either wooden or glass-topped tables and some stainless steel. No matter what type of tables you choose, whether they are glass tops, wooden or laminate, make sure that they are easy to clean and fit in with the rest of your décor.

Comfortable chairs are a must. I always think high bar stools are really uncomfortable and I would always avoid them when possible.

Some attractive pictures on the walls and a few large plants will add the finishing touches to your coffee shop.

Flooring

Think carefully when you are buying flooring for the sitting area in your coffee shop; there are many types on the market now. You should choose something that is hard-wearing and easy to keep clean because you are bound to have some spillage.

There are some excellent designs available and some of the more expensive makes come with a 20-year guarantee. However, if you have a large area to cover, you might want to consider something cheaper. Laminate or hardwood flooring are popular but if they get wet they can warp over time.

Floor tiles appear to be the best option as they are hard-wearing and easy to clean. They are permanent and if they are of good quality they shouldn't chip easily. You can choose self-coloured or speckled tiles. The speckled ones don't show the dirt as quickly.

Carpet tiles are warm, can be vacuumed and the tiles can be replaced one by one. If you are going to use carpet tiles make sure you purchase extra tiles to replace any that become stained. I wouldn't recommend a carpet because it is difficult to clean well and there is no doubt that it will quickly become stained with coffee and food.

Cleanliness

No matter what the style of your coffee shop, cleanliness is of paramount importance. Always make sure your staff wipe the tables when they clear them of dirty dishes. If they are busy they may find it easier simply to remove the used crockery. This gives a dreadful impression and is a practice which must be discouraged.

Many customers judge a coffee shop or restaurant by the toilets. Pleasant washrooms with nice soap and paper towels create a good impression. Have a rota for staff to check the toilets during opening hours to ensure that they are clean and that there is always a ready supply of toilet tissue and paper towels.

It is advisable to fix your soap dispensers to the wall as, unfortunately, soap tends to disappear. And sometimes children who are allowed to go to the washroom on their own will make a game of scooting the soap all over the walls and floor. (Yes, it does happen – on more than one occasion in our coffee shop toilets.)

Do place a large enough waste bin in the wash-basin area because overflowing bins look unsightly.

DEVISING A STAFF UNIFORM

The image projected by your staff is very important in helping to ensure the success of your coffee shop. Customers prefer to be served food and drink by someone who looks neat, clean and smartly dressed. A uniform conveys professionalism and helps to reinforce your coffee shop's identity.

The benefits for staff are that they are saved the expense of buying clothing for work and they also don't have to think about what they are going to wear each day. However, it's important that staff know that you are sensitive to their needs so you must provide them with uniforms that, as well as looking good, are also comfortable, practical and easy to wear.

Your basic uniform could consist of the following:

☐ an apron;

☐ a shirt, polo shirt or smart T-shirt;

☐ black trousers.

If you like, you could include a neck tie/scarf or a cap.

Aprons

You will need a good supply of these. They are essential for waiting staff who will undoubtedly spill tea or coffee on them during the day. Dark colours are best as they will disguise stains more effectively. Black is a favourite colour and is easy to find in any workwear shop.

Aprons with bibs are more practical as they provide protection against splashes from coffee and tea. However, younger staff and male staff tend to prefer a bib-less, knee length or below the knee length apron. Aprons should also be made of a heavy material, be machine washable and non iron.

You can have the name of your coffee shop and your logo, if you have one, printed on the aprons. This can be done either by having the items embroidered or by using an iron-on transfer. There are companies who will do this for you but try to negotiate a good price. Uniform suppliers may be able to put your logo on a wide variety of clothing in your chosen colour.

 It is a good idea to wash the aprons belonging to your staff yourself as they tend to lose them by leaving them on the train or the bus. It is a bit of a nuisance but saves you money in the long run. If you have a washing machine/dryer on the premises, all the better but, if not, either take them home with you to wash, or send them to the laundry.

Remember, you will also use a few dozen tea towels and dish cloths in the kitchen each day that will also have to be washed or sent to the laundry. You will save a lot of money by doing them yourself but you may be able to negotiate with your local laundry service and agree a reduced price for guaranteeing them the business for a certain period of time.

Shirts

You could opt for either an easy to iron shirt, a polo shirt or a T-shirt. Short-sleeved shirts work best because long sleeves tend to get dirty quite quickly when wiping and clearing tables.

A white shirt, when new, always looks crisp and clean and looks good with black trousers and a black apron. Remember though that when it has been washed a number of times it could appear grey and dingy so it may be better to choose a colour instead. A check or striped shirt also looks smart and does not show stains as much as a self colour does.

You could also try to link the uniform to your logo by picking out a colour from your logo and matching all the shirts to that particular colour. Alternatively, you could have your logo embroidered on the pockets of the shirts, or have a transfer of your logo ironed onto the shirts.

Trousers

Black trousers or a black skirt always look smart, will go with any colour of shirt and are easy to keep clean.

Even if you decide not to supply your staff with uniforms you must stipulate what they should wear. Inappropriate dress such as bare midriffs or low-cut necklines on female staff will be off-putting to most customers.

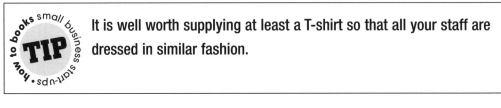

It is well worth supplying at least a T-shirt so that all your staff are dressed in similar fashion.

Insist on your staff coming to work wearing clean, pressed clothes and shoes that are polished and in good repair.

Ask both female and male staff to tie long hair back. This is more hygienic and looks neat and tidy.

Making the most of your menu

Your printed menu is extremely important; it shows your customers exactly what you have to offer. You can have the menu printed with your name and logo on the front and everything you are selling inside.

Don't have too many menus printed initially as you will need to have them reprinted when you change your prices. You may also want to add new items to your menu or delete certain ones which you recognize are not selling well.

Care must be taken when planning your menu. It should reflect what you can cope with so don't get too ambitious. Keep it simple; it is better to offer less to start with and build up a more comprehensive menu after being in business for a while.

You should have a daily specials board, either one mounted on the wall or a sandwich board. As well as listing specials on this board, you should look ahead and if a dish or a filling is not selling as fast as you would like, add it to the specials board and reduce the price. It is better to get some profit from it while it is still fresh rather than having to throw it away when it is past its sell by date.

Most coffee shops offer soup, light bites and home baking. You could simply offer soup of the day on your menu and specify what soup it will be for that day on your specials board. Soup always sells well, even in the summer, and you can make a good profit from it.

List paninis, toasted sandwiches, sandwiches and filled rolls, together with the fillings available. On your menu print the most common fillings but put one or two more unusual fillings on your daily specials board. You will then be able to see what your customers like without committing yourself to offering these fillings every day. Try to give as much detail as possible for your fillings. Don't just list cheese and ham, for instance; find out where the cheese comes from and what type of ham it is and describe your filling as, for example, Orkney Cheddar Cheese with Honey Roast Ham. Your ingredients will sound much more appealing and suggestive of quality if you say 'Scottish Smoked Salmon and Philadelphia Cream Cheese', or 'Egg Mayonnaise made from Organic Eggs and the best Creamy Mayonnaise'. (See Chapter 5 for more details on menus.)

Print out a suggestion sheet for your customers to propose fillings or other food they would like you to offer. You could also ask them to make general comments and recommendations. This feedback is invaluable as it will help you improve your business. See Appendix 6 for an example of a customer questionnaire.

Next you should list all your speciality coffees, teas including fruit and herbal teas, hot chocolate and cold drinks. Remember to list children's beverages, including sugar-free drinks.

Be aware of what is popular and keep up with trends by reading food magazines and visiting other good coffee shops when time permits.

Don't ever sell anything that is past its sell by date. If you do you could jeopardise your business.

Don't use chalk to write on your specials board because you will find that children will rub off your menu as soon as you turn your back. Use a dry marker pen instead. You can purchase them in various bright colours and children won't be able to rub the writing off the board.

PRICING YOUR MENU

One of the most difficult tasks is establishing prices that will cover your overheads and give you a profit.

In order to work out your prices you will need to calculate the cost of each item by adding up the cost of all the ingredients in the recipe and taking into account the time it took to make the item. Some items will be less expensive and less time consuming to make than others. For example, a carrot cake takes longer and is more expensive to make than a plain sponge. I would recommend you lower your profit on the carrot cake and increase your profit on the plain sponge and sell them both at the same price.

In general you should work on achieving a 60% profit although you may be guided by what your competitors are charging. If your prices are higher than those of your competitors, you may find that customers will be prepared to pay a bit more if you are offering something special; for example, good service, a friendly atmosphere or great coffee and home baking.

In our coffee shop we work on a 50% gross profit because we opt for a large volume at lower prices. However, some small exclusive coffee shops work on low volume with high prices.

Always aim to give your customers value for money. People expect to pay a fair price for good coffee and good food.

Size matters! I know of a most successful coffee/teashop in the Highlands of Scotland, close to a railway station and also on the main road into one of the few large(ish) towns for many miles around. The customer profile is a mixture of passing tourists, local ladies who meet for coffee or tea and those from a wider area who from time to time drive past the shop on their way into the town for provisions. The teashop is famous for its scones. Few who visit fail to return, as the scones are just magnificent. The coffee shop offers three varieties – plain, fruit and cheese. They are all so good that customers sometimes struggle to select which one they want. Then one day the owners had a mental aberration and decided to offer two sizes of scone. They dithered over whether to call them 'large' and 'small' or 'standard' and 'large'. Finally they settled on 'scones' and 'large scones' and had their menus printed. Within a week the table staff were on the point of industrial action. They were being driven demented as customers who already couldn't decide what type of scone to have now wanted to know just how large a 'large scone' was. Some customers decided to share a large scone and some argued that the large scone on one plate wasn't all that much bigger than the standard scone on another plate. It took twice as long for the staff to take a simple order. The following week the menus were reprinted once again and – lo- only one size of scone appeared!

The moral of this story is that it is better to try out new ideas for a while before changing your menu, because if it doesn't work, you won't have incurred the expense of having to get your menu reprinted.

Should you opt for self-service or table service?

This is a personal choice though I believe it depends on the location and size of your coffee shop. If you have a large seating area I think, on balance, it is better to have self-service because:

☐ you will save money on the cost of waiting staff;

☐ you can make sure that everyone has paid for their order before receiving it. Customers then shouldn't be able to walk out without paying.

Even though we have self-service in our coffee shop, on one occasion a customer took a cake and slid it around the corner so that the person taking her money didn't see it and therefore didn't charge her for it. When it was discovered that she had done this, it was too late and she had eaten the evidence!

If you have a small coffee shop, table service is best because:

☐ your customers receive better customer care;

☐ customers enjoy the attention they get from their waiter/waitress;

☐ customers will probably order more from the waiting staff;

☐ waiting staff can boost your profits by promoting your food and drink. They can suggest to your customers that they try a particular sandwich, cake or coffee that they think tastes great;

☐ your staff receive more tips when they give table service.

Americans mostly favour self-service but the British are more formal and prefer table service. Urban likes self-service – rural likes table service.

Deciding your opening hours

You will have to decide what are the optimum opening hours for your premises. This depends not only on the area in which you are situated but also on your customer profile.

Our coffee shop is situated within a retail shop, therefore we open the coffee shop at the same time as the retail shop, which is 10 a.m. We close the coffee shop at 5 p.m. to allow the staff time to clean the sitting area, toilets and kitchen before the retail shop closes at 6 p.m.

If you are in an area where the other shops open at 9 a.m. you may want to open at 8.30 a.m. to catch people going to work; and if you are going to sell hot bacon or egg rolls for breakfast you may also want to open early. Most people are going home at around 5 p.m. so you would probably want to close at that time to allow your staff to clean up ready for the next day.

No matter what hours you decide to open your shop, you will have to be there yourself early in the morning to take in deliveries of milk, bread and rolls, fresh vegetables and other orders. Also if you are going to bake your own scones and cakes you will probably have to start around 7 a.m. so that you are prepared for opening.

> *When we first started our coffee shop I honestly thought that I would only have to arrive at work about half an hour before opening time. How wrong I was. I start at 6 a.m. to take in all the deliveries, set up the coffee machine and start baking!*

You have to be able to prepare yourself for an early start unless you have a good manager who will do all these jobs for you. However, most people can't afford to take on a manager when they first start their business. As long as you are in good health, are physically fit and you are passionate about what you do, it won't feel like work.

5
DEVISING YOUR MENU

Creating the menu for your coffee shop is one of your most important tasks. You will need to consider carefully what type of food and which hot and cold beverages you are going to serve.

Catering to suit your customer

You will need to cater for the particular type of customer base in your area. For example, if your coffee shop is located in a less affluent area, you should create your menu to suit your customers' pockets, but perhaps include a daily special which is more unusual. Conversely, if your location is in a more affluent district, you may be able to include more up-market ingredients.

You will probably have tried many varieties of sandwich, panini and baked potato while you were doing your research, but try to be objective as your customers won't necessarily enjoy the same food as you do. If you concentrate on a range of basic or core fillings and introduce one or two special dishes or fillings of the day for your sandwiches and baked potatoes, you will soon get to know what your customers like.

 Don't make too large a quantity of a new item until you see how your customers like it or you will risk throwing away more than you sell. It is always better to run out of something rather than have to throw it away!

Serving cold-filled snacks and sandwiches
COLD FILLINGS

It is a good idea to offer several cold fillings for paninis, toasted sandwiches, sandwiches and baked potatoes. Some of those that I have found to be popular are:

- ☐ tuna mayonnaise;

- ☐ chicken mayonnaise or chicken and sweetcorn;

- ☐ coronation chicken or chicken tikka;

- ☐ cheese, ham and tomato;

- ☐ cheese and pickle;

- egg mayonnaise;

- prawns, naked or with a Marie Rose sauce;

- BLT (bacon, lettuce and tomato).

More unusual fillings for your daily special

If you want to experiment with more unusual fillings to try out on your customers as daily specials, check out other coffee shops and recipe books to give you some ideas. In Chapter 12 I have included some suggestions for fillings which have proved popular with my customers. In addition, I have listed below a few fillings which I have tried and found to be successful:

- smoked salmon and cream cheese;

- corned beef with mayonnaise, spring onion and tomato;

- chicken and cranberry sauce and mayonnaise;

- peanut butter and banana (might appeal to vegetarians);

- lobster meat with mayonnaise and cayenne pepper;

- avocado and Brie or another cheese (again might appeal to vegetarians);

- roast beef and horseradish;

- cream cheese or cottage cheese with crisp bacon or ham.

Do try to make up your fillings fresh in the morning and keep them in the fridge to use as required. Also prepare fresh tubs of salad every morning for garnishing and using in sandwiches. You could also offer a variety of salads that can be made up to order based around your sandwich ingredients – and you could also include a special salad on your menu.

MAKING SANDWICHES AND ROLLS TO ORDER

It really is better to make your sandwiches to order as customers prefer to see their sandwich freshly made to their own specification. Also, you will have less waste at the end of the day. Simply offer a choice of bread available and a selection of fillings which can be priced by having an extra key especially for fillings on your till.

Garnishes

Whichever sandwich or baked potato you are serving, a salad garnish makes it look much more appetizing and professional. We always serve our sandwiches with a salad garnish and crisps but you can decide yourself what garnish looks best. Again, when doing your research of other coffee shops, take note of what garnish they use and what looks more appealing to you.

 Mayonnaise is used in most sandwiches because it tastes good and makes the sandwich moist. However not everyone wants mayonnaise – especially if they are watching the calories – so do keep some cooked chicken and prawns aside so that you can offer mayonnaise-free sandwiches.

MAKING YOUR SANDWICHES IN ADVANCE

Filled sandwiches can, of course, be made in advance and wrapped in cling film to keep them fresh. If you want to do this, make a small selection to begin with to see how well they sell. The downside of this is that the filled sandwiches/rolls have not only to be wrapped separately but also to be individually labelled. This takes up a lot of time. Also, the filled sandwiches/rolls take up precious room, unless you have chilled counters with a lot of space.

You could, of course, buy in ready-made sandwiches but I personally do not think this would entice people into your coffee shop as they can buy this type of sandwich in super-markets or other outlets.

OFFERING A VARIETY OF BREADS

There are so many different types of bread and rolls on the market now, such as:

- ☐ mixed grain;

- ☐ poppy seed;

- ☐ ciabatta;

- ☐ focaccia;

- ☐ bagels;

to name but a few.

In my experience, a large number of customers still like ordinary sliced white and brown bread or rolls. So do offer a basic white and brown pan loaf and experiment with a few of the more unusual types until you discover what your customers like. Then you can add these to your menu. It is really trial and error to begin with and again I would recommend only buying a small quantity of different breads otherwise you could end up throwing away your profit as well as the bread at the end of the day!

Fresh is best

One of the important skills you will learn, occasionally the hard way, is to purchase only the perishable food that you actually require. You can, of course, freeze surplus bread at the end of the day and use it at a later date; it is always advisable to freeze a small amount of bread just in case you are extremely busy and run out of fresh bread. To retain freshness, bread must be frozen and never refrigerated. Generally, of course, I prefer to use fresh bread and rolls daily, but a good way to use up your defrosted bread is to use it for toast and toasted sandwiches.

Getting your daily bread

Suppliers are keen to give you free samples of their bread so take advantage of this as it will allow you to discover what type of bread and rolls your customers prefer. Try to get a supplier who will deliver your rolls and bread daily. Alternatively, you could buy them from the supermarket in the morning before opening your shop. It may be less expensive to do this at first and you can decide each morning what quantity you will need. The downside to this is that it will take up your time in the morning before you go to work. Remember, you will have to start early – 6 a.m. – 7 a.m. – to get all your deliveries in and do all your preparations, baking, etc. prior to opening time.

Serving hot-filled snacks and sandwiches

Baked potatoes and paninis are very popular and can be made with hot or cold fillings. For baked potatoes you can use some of the cold fillings listed above and also a variety of hot fillings listed below. See also Chapter 12 for more ideas for fillings. Popular hot fillings include:

- chilli con carne;
- curry;
- haggis;
- cheese and coleslaw;
- baked beans and cheese;
- creamed mushrooms;
- macaroni and cheese.

QUICHE

I find that, in the summer, home-made quiche is a great favourite with customers. I serve it hot or cold, with salad or salad garnish and chips. Quiche is easy to make and is a profitable meal to serve. You can choose a variety of fillings but always include at least one that is suitable for vegetarians.

Making your own soup

Home-made soup is also very popular and in fact is one of the best selling items on our menu. When we first opened our coffee shop we made one large 8-pint pot of traditional soup which sold well but now that we are established we sell approximately 5 gallons of traditional soup and 8 pints of cream soup per day. We give a good-sized bowl of soup (two ladlesful) along with a slice of fresh crusty bread and butter or a fresh roll and butter. Don't be tempted to use up yesterday's bread as your customers will notice and will think you are not giving value for money. Nor should you use packet or tinned soup – there is no comparison to good home-made soup.

 **Remember, you will have some customers who are vegetarian, so advertise your vegetable soups as being suitable for vegetarians, and make sure no meat stock has been used in them.**

Here are some of the most popular soups that I serve in our coffee shop:

- □ lentil;
- □ chicken and rice;
- □ leek and potato;
- □ broth;
- □ chicken noodle;
- □ minestrone.

You can also offer a cream soup daily (make a smaller pot as not everyone likes cream soups). The following are popular with my customers:

- □ cream of mushroom;
- □ cream of chicken;
- □ cream of carrot and coriander;
- □ cream of parsnip and curry;
- □ cream of cauliflower or broccoli and stilton;
- □ cream of sweet potato and chilli;
- □ cullen skink (a Scottish soup made from smoked haddock and cream).

 Offer a combination of a bowl of soup plus a filled sandwich at a specially reduced price. And for children you could offer half a bowl of soup plus a small sandwich.

You could also offer cartons of soup to carry out as this suits people in a hurry at lunchtime, who don't have time to sit in and eat.

You will find some of my soup recipes in Chapter 12.

Serving breakfasts

If you decide to serve breakfasts it is advisable to give a cut-off time – say, 11.30 a.m. – or you will get caught up in trying to cook breakfasts and serve lunches at the same time, which is not ideal. However, if you do have space and time, you could offer an all-day breakfast.

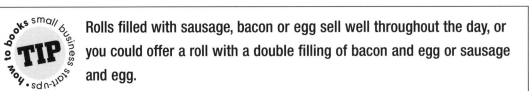 **Rolls filled with sausage, bacon or egg sell well throughout the day, or you could offer a roll with a double filling of bacon and egg or sausage and egg.**

Scrambled eggs on toast and beans on toast are easy and quick to make and there is a good profit margin on these simple dishes.

A recipe I picked up from a friend in the USA is a Breakfast Casserole which is a bit different from the traditional English Breakfast and tastes delicious. It can be prepared the day before and put into the fridge and cooked the next morning. Portions can be served with toast or crusty bread. See Chapter 12 for the recipe.

Serving home-cooked meals

Should you decide to increase your menu to include home-cooked meals you could try some of the following, but remember not to make too much at first until you see what you can sell in a day. You could make one or two interesting meals as special items on your menu until your business is established and you know what type of food your customers are looking for.

WELL KNOWN FAVOURITES

Home-made lasagne is still very popular and if you make a large tray of it you can freeze some of the portions for use at a later date.

Unless you have an upmarket coffee shop, fish and chips, scampi, mince and potatoes, braised sausage, and steak pie are still old favourites with customers. Chilli con carne or curry served with rice or chips, and pasta bolognaise also sell well. However, it is important to make all these recipes on the premises and not to buy in frozen substitutes. If you make the food yourself, your coffee shop will get a reputation for serving good home-made food at a reasonable price. Customers want value for money.

MORE ADVENTUROUS FARE

If you do have an upmarket coffee shop and you decide to include cooked meals, the sky is the limit and you can make a variety of unusual and interesting meals from your own recipes or from recipes you have collected when doing your research. You can also include a few of the old favourites.

Catering for children

Young couples will probably frequent your coffee shop and it is advisable to offer meals for their children. You can do this by buying in such things as fish fingers, chicken burgers and small pizzas. You can also offer children's portions of the food you are making for adults.

PORTION SIZES

However, be aware that offering children's portions can cause problems. Some adults may be tempted to order a child's meal because it is cheaper and the portion can be almost as large as the adult portion! This can lead to a delicate situation – and you must avoid disputes with your customers. You must have a clear policy. You could ensure that your kitchen staff serve a half-sized portion for half the price, unless you do not mind adults purchasing a child's meal even though it cuts down on your profit.

Beef, chicken and vegetable burgers are favourites with children and teenagers, and can be topped with cheese, fried onions or egg, and served with a salad garnish or chips. They are easy to make as you can cook them from frozen, or indeed you can make your own fresh burgers.

ICE CREAM AND ICE LOLLIES

If you have room for a freezer, you may want to consider selling ice creams and ice lollies. Ice cream companies will sometimes provide you with a freezer on loan, or free, if you agree to sell their products. If this is what you want to do then contact a few companies to find out what deals they can offer you. They may also discount your first order or they may give you a longer period of credit before you have to pay for the stock. Do bear in mind though that freezers take up a lot of space, and while you probably won't sell many ice creams in the winter, you will have money tied up in keeping your freezer well stocked. Think carefully before making a decision about offering ices on your menu.

Baking your own cakes

If you want to attract customers to your coffee shop home baking is a must. Always try to bake your own cakes and tray bakes on the premises as your customers will be able to tell the difference. Alternatively, you could purchase cakes from someone who bakes them at home, providing the baker is registered with the Environmental Health Department of your local council. In our coffee shop we sell over 150 cakes and tray bakes a day, and on a Saturday we sell about 200 cakes and tray bakes, all of which are home-baked on the premises.

Last year we had a problem with our oven and couldn't use it for four days. We bought in bakes but our customers complained about the size of the portions and the lack of variety. Our cakes and tray bakes are always a generous portion and our customers are used to that. It is important always to be consistent in portion size and quality. People do really appreciate home-made cakes and tray bakes and not all coffee shops provide these, so it really is worth making it a priority. But always find out where you can purchase bakery just in case you have to do so in an emergency.

FAVOURITE CAKES

I have listed below some of our customers' favourite cakes. Some I put out every day as they are consistently good sellers and others I offer occasionally as specials. I usually offer a choice of 12 to 14 cakes including tray bakes each day but it is better to offer a smaller selection until you get established.

 Remember to give your customers a good portion, a good choice and value for money, and you can't go wrong.

Everyday favourites
- ☐ Apple Pie
- ☐ Doughnuts
- ☐ Fruit Loaf
- ☐ Fudge Slice
- ☐ Mars Bar Crispy Cake
- ☐ Millionaire Shortbread
- ☐ Plain Sponge
- ☐ Rhubarb Pie
- ☐ Scones with Butter
- ☐ Scones with Cream and Jam
- ☐ Scottish Butter Shortbread

Occasional 'specials'

- ☐ Apple, Cinnamon and Chocolate Chip Cake
- ☐ Banana, Cranberry and Nut Loaf
- ☐ Banoffee Pie
- ☐ Carrot Cake
- ☐ Chocolate Cake
- ☐ Coconut Slice
- ☐ Crispy Surprise
- ☐ Cup Cakes
- ☐ Empire Biscuits
- ☐ Gingerbread
- ☐ Lemon Cheesecake
- ☐ Lemon Slice
- ☐ Malteser Slice
- ☐ Meringues
- ☐ Mint Slice
- ☐ Muffins
- ☐ Key Lime Pie
- ☐ Scottish Tablet
- ☐ Sticky Toffee Buns
- ☐ Strawberry Tarts

I always make scones and doughnuts first thing in the morning so that they are fresh and ready to serve when we open. Home-made meringues are a fantastic seller and I could sell them all every day but as they take a long time to cook at a low temperature it is not always possible to monopolise the oven for that length of time.

Some coffee shops also offer a range of desserts, for example, sticky toffee pudding, bread and butter pudding, apple crumble. However, this requires time and the use of your microwave oven, possibly at the busiest time of the day, which is not always possible. Again, it is a case of trial and error, and you could do well with old favourite desserts and also a few new, exciting ones.

Once again, I have included some of my recipes in Chapter 12.

Offering a choice of hot and cold drinks

COFFEE

We serve the following coffees in our coffee shop:

☐ cappuccino;

☐ filter coffee;

☐ espresso;

☐ latte coffee (plain or flavoured with vanilla or caramel);

☐ mocha;

☐ Nescafé decaf.

Before deciding on which ground coffee and coffee beans you are going to use in your shop, visit other coffee shops, sample theirs and, if you like it, ask the name of their supplier. Usually suppliers will give you samples of coffee to try before you decide which one you think would appeal to your customers. We like Matthew Algie coffee and I have given the contact details in the Chapter 6.

If you don't want the expense of purchasing an espresso coffee machine it is possible to lease one from your coffee supplier.

Don't install a coffee machine that does everything at the press of a button as these automatic machines usually use powdered coffee and powdered milk. In my opinion there is no comparison to the flavour of coffee made in an authentic espresso coffee machine, which uses freshly ground coffee beans and fresh milk. Don't let anyone persuade you otherwise. You can make cappuccino, mocha, white coffee and black coffee. Hot chocolate can also be made using powdered chocolate and fresh steamed milk.

TEA

Using a good-quality tea is a must although, if you want to make a larger profit, you can purchase a less expensive tea. However, your customers may not enjoy it as much.

Offer Earl Grey tea and a choice of flavoured and herbal teas as these are very popular with some customers.

COLD DRINKS

Offer a good choice of diet, non-diet drinks and sugar-free drinks. Find out what drinks are popular and include them in your selection. Also keep a good range of drinks suitable for children. The following is a good selection to offer:

□ Pepsi or Coca-Cola;

□ Fanta Lemon and Fanta Orange;

□ Iron Bru (a Scottish favourite);

□ Sprite;

□ carbonated flavoured water;

□ still flavoured water;

□ still natural water;

□ a selection of children's drinks and juices.

Try offering milk shakes made with flavoured syrups plus ice cream, or simply flavoured milk. You can buy flavoured milk in cartons or you can make it up yourself with syrup in a blender. It only takes seconds and there is more profit to be made in the one you make up yourself.

Smoothies are very popular with health-conscious customers and also children, but unless you have time to juice fruit yourself I would advise buying in ready-made cartons or bottles.

 **Make sure your staff know that when they fill the drinks chiller they must always bring the older drinks to the front in order that you are not left with out-of-date cans and bottles. Staff sometimes overlook this when the coffee shop is busy, but you must impress upon them how important it is.**

Remember to keep a stock of drinking straws as some customers prefer to have a straw with the bottle instead of a glass, and most children love to have a straw in their drink.

You will be surprised how many customers are on diets and request sweeteners for their coffee and tea as an alternative to sugar, so it is a good idea to have a supply available.

A university student who worked for us at weekends and in the holidays came to me one day to ask if a serviette was a sweetener! A customer had asked her for a serviette and she thought it was another name for Sweetex.

6
PURCHASING AND LEASING CATERING EQUIPMENT

You can choose either to purchase or lease most equipment, but in some cases it is better to lease.

Buying new equipment

We started our coffee shop from scratch and had to buy everything. Having no experience in this type of business, it was trial and error.

If you can afford it, you should always try to purchase new equipment. When you buy new you usually get one year's guarantee, so you will have peace of mind for that year. Keep all your guarantees and manuals in a file for easy access because you never know when you might have to have a piece of equipment repaired.

Before investing money on new or second-hand equipment, you should do your homework thoroughly. Talk to other coffee shop or restaurant owners to see what equipment they prefer to have, and why. Also check the internet to see if there is any information on the item of equipment you are considering purchasing.

> *We have had to have our food mixer repaired three times since we bought it. The first time it was still under the guarantee, but on the other two occasions we had to pay for the repair and the postage.*

If you are taking over an already established business you should have all the fittings and fixtures included in the sale or lease and the kitchen should already be fitted out. This will save you purchasing a lot of expensive items initially and, hopefully, you should not need to replace any large items until you have made enough profit to do so.

 It is said that catering equipment only lasts approximately five to six years, especially if you are going to open your coffee shop six or seven days a week. It is advisable therefore to plan to renew an item every five years.

Buying second-hand equipment

If you are working to a tight budget you can often purchase second-hand and reconditioned equipment at a good price from auction sales, dealers or from shops that are closing down.

Sometimes it is worth buying second-hand as it can save you a lot of money. Remember, you may have to transport the equipment that you have purchased. You might have to hire a van or pay a delivery charge, so take the cost of that into account.

> *I know a coffee shop owner, working on a limited budget, who purchased all his tables and chairs second-hand for £60 at an auction. He was delighted with his purchases and simply covered the tables with pretty oilcloth tablecloths. I'm sure you will agree that this purchase saved him quite a lot of money. He also bought most of his kitchen equipment and fitments second-hand and so far he hasn't had any problems with them.*

TIP *how to books small business start-ups*

Buyer, beware: if you decide to buy any equipment through classified advertisements, at an auction, or from a dealer who is not reputable, then take great care as you will not have any guarantee with these items. If your budget is tight, you will have to be ready to take a chance, but do your homework first. Go to see the item before you buy, if that is possible. Ask how old it is and if you can test it to see if it is working. Also, ask if there have been any repairs done to the item and, if so, what they were, and how much they cost. Better still, if you know someone who has some knowledge about the equipment you are considering purchasing, take that person with you to check it out.

Buying or leasing kitchen equipment

There are companies who will design and install your kitchen for you and, if you are going to go down this road, do get several quotations before you make a final decision. You will be able to search for these companies on the internet and also look in the Yellow Pages.

Before you buy or lease any equipment do try to visit other commercial kitchens to see their layouts. Ask the owners or managers what equipment they think is essential. I have listed the kitchen equipment which I think is essential and I have included some items which I think are desirable.

Upgrading or fitting a commercial kitchen can be expensive, so you could consider leasing instead of purchasing your equipment.

ESPRESSO COFFEE MACHINE

Purchasing or leasing the right coffee machine is very important because if you don't serve good coffee your customers won't return.

A good authentic coffee machine is very expensive to purchase and you will have to sell an awful lot of coffees to cover the cost. We did our research and decided to lease our coffee machine. We also entered into a maintenance agreement. At the time you will think that a maintenance agreement seems to be an expensive outlay but in the event that your coffee machine breaks down during a busy period you will be thankful that you made the investment. We found that it was advantageous because the company we lease from guarantee to send an engineer to the customer's premises as soon as possible after they report a breakdown.

The company you lease your machine from will come to your shop and give your staff training on making different types of coffee, and instructions on how to keep the machine clean.

We lease an Elektra Maxi Espresso Coffee Machine from Matthew Algie. It costs approximately £100 per month to lease but you can lease a smaller one for about £80 per month. This amount also includes a precision coffee grinder and the cost of the maintenance. Matthew Algie offer staff training in their Coffee School and on your premises.

We also purchase our coffee beans, ground coffee and flavoured syrups from Matthew Algie as they offer a next-day delivery service. You can look at their website which is www.matthewalgie.co.uk and can telephone them on 0141 429 2817.

It is essential that you clean the hot milk wand after each use or the milk will harden onto the wand and it will be difficult to clean at the end of the day. You should also ensure that you clean your machine on a daily basis to the manufacturer's instructions because failure to do so causes a build-up of oily residue in the pipes which gives the coffee a bitter taste.

FILTER COFFEE MACHINE

I would also advise you to get a filter coffee machine, firstly, because some people prefer filter coffee; and, secondly, because if your espresso machine breaks down you can offer filter coffee to your customers until your other machine is repaired. If you don't want to go to the expense of purchasing a filter coffee machine (which could cost you around £100), companies that lease machines will usually be able to supply you with one free on loan as long as you agree to purchase their ground coffee.

COFFEE GRINDER

A coffee grinder is essential. You will need to grind the coffee beans to use in your coffee machine. You can get a grinder from the company you are leasing your coffee machine from. If you were to purchase a coffee grinder it would cost you approximately £380 so, if you can include this in your lease agreement, it is worthwhile.

WATER BOILER

You will require constant boiling water to make pots of tea so a water boiler is essential. It saves you time because the water is always at the correct temperature and you don't have to wait for a kettle to boil. A manual-fill water boiler will cost around £117. You can purchase a boiler which is plumbed in, but they are more expensive, costing from around £235. They are much more convenient but you will have to get a plumber to connect it to the mains water supply. You can get water boilers in different sizes from 5 litres to 20 litres.

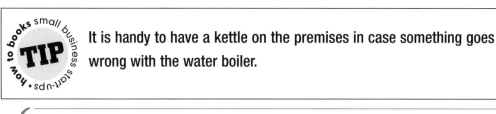

It is handy to have a kettle on the premises in case something goes wrong with the water boiler.

> *On two occasions the thermostat in our water boiler has burned out. We had to use a kettle and the espresso machine until the engineer replaced the thermostat.*

Most coffee machines will give you instant boiling water. I have found that this is all right in an emergency, but if you use them continually for this purpose, you will have to wait for the steam to build up again before you can make another cappuccino or café latte.

It is necessary to have the espresso machine and your water boiler plumbed in because they fill automatically and the excess water has to be drained.

DISHWASHER

Dishwashers are preferable to manual washing and are said to be more economical and very efficient at disinfecting dishes, cutlery, pots and pans and small items of equipment.

A good commercial dishwasher is both a must and a godsend. The washing cycle takes a fraction of the time a domestic dishwasher takes; it can be set to take one, two or three minutes to wash the dishes. We set our dishwasher for the three-minute cycle. You fill the basket neatly so that items do not overlap and then place it in the dishwasher, close the lid and three minutes later the dishes are washed. You will be surprised at the amount of dishes you can wash at one time.

You can purchase a commercial dishwasher from around £1,700 including VAT, or you can lease one from about £12 per week.

We did invest in a spray which is situated over the sink to rinse off the excess food before washing the dishes in the machine. This piece of equipment is not essential but I would recommend purchasing one if you can afford it.

Follow the manufacturer's recommendations for loading and using your dishwasher. Rinse any large particles of food off the dishes before you put them in the machine. You will find that you also have to scrub your pots before putting them in the dishwasher.

You will have to use a good commercial dishwasher liquid, and a rinse aid which is fed into the machine automatically and which is approved by the Environmental Health Agency.

WASTE DISPOSAL SYSTEM

A waste disposal in the sink is not essential but it is excellent for getting rid of left-over food. Alternatively you could place a small bin with a plastic liner inserted in it beside the sink to scrape the left-over food off the dishes before putting them into the dishwasher.

We have found that a large majority of people won't eat salad and it comes back untouched and has to be thrown away. This is certainly wasteful but food looks so much better presented with a garnish.

FREEZER

You will find that commercial freezers are expensive to purchase but they are built to withstand the hash and bash of the kitchen staff. We store frozen paninis, bread, chips, fish, meat and chicken, as well as ice cream and some bakery.

Do remember to place thermometers in your freezers so that you can maintain the correct temperature to keep food fresh.

REFRIGERATOR

Commercial fridges are also expensive but are built to withstand the number of times the door has to be opened and closed during a busy working day. A fridge which displays its temperature on the outside is beneficial because you can make sure that it is at the correct temperature at all times (1°C to 4°C). You will have to record these readings on your temperature chart twice a day, in the morning and in the afternoon. If your fridges don't have a visible temperature display, make sure that you place thermometers inside them.

You will probably want to have an upright fridge cooler for your cold drinks. If you don't want to purchase a drinks cooler, some drinks companies will supply them free of charge as long as you purchase their brand of drinks.

FOOD DISPLAY UNIT

You will require a chilled food display unit if you are going to display cream cakes or ready-made sandwiches. You can also purchase a display unit which is not chilled to display cakes and confectionery at an ambient temperature.

 If you are not going to sell ready-made sandwiches or cream cakes you should choose the ordinary display unit because the chilled version will make the edges of your sponges and cakes hard.

 Do purchase a display case that is not self-service because you will find that some customers will lift the cakes and in some instances feel them with their fingers before making a final choice.

COOKER

You should invest in a good commercial oven because a domestic oven will not withstand the abuse it will have to take.

I personally think a gas oven and burners are better than an electric oven and burners because the heat is instant and you can control it. A double oven is a must if you are going to do your own baking on the premises. You can choose either four or six burners but, if you have space, I would opt for six burners.

You can purchase a four-burner range cooker for about £1,200 or lease one for around £9 per week. A six-burner range cooker will cost you around £1,500 to buy, or you can lease one for around £11.50 per week.

BAIN-MARIE

If you are going to serve hot food a bain-marie is a convenient way of holding hot vegetables, beans, soup, macaroni cheese and other foods. It has thermostatic control which allows you to keep the food at the required temperature.

GRILL

A high-level grill is a must because you can keep an eye on what is grilling without having to bend down all the time.

PANINI GRILL

This is a heavy-duty contact grill to use for making paninis but you can also make toasted sandwiches on it. It takes a little while to heat up so turn it on in the morning and leave it on until after your lunchtime rush.

> *Paninis are one of our best sellers so the panini grill has been a really worthwhile piece of equipment in our kitchen; it has paid for itself many times over.*

Think very carefully before you enter into the type of contract that ties you into buying a company's products. You can, for instance, get a free oven which cooks part-baked paninis and various pastries from a well-known company but you have to agree to take a certain amount of their produce every week. When you have just started in business, you do not know how many paninis and pastries you will be able to sell per week.

GRIDDLE

A griddle is excellent if you are going to be serving quite a lot of bacon, eggs, sausage and burgers and also if you have space to install it. It saves time messing around with frying pans. If you have a griddle you should turn it on first thing in the morning as it takes a considerable time to heat up.

> *I know a coffee shop owner who serves rolls filled with sausage, bacon, egg and burgers, and they get into such a mess because they have to use a frying pan each time they get an order. Unfortunately, they don't have room to install a griddle.*

MICROWAVE

A good commercial microwave is essential; you will be amazed at how useful you will find it. Initially, we started off with two microwaves but have recently bought another one.

If you are going to offer scrambled egg on your menu, always cook it in the microwave as it saves cleaning dirty scrambled egg pots.

TOASTED SANDWICH MAKER

Do purchase a toasted sandwich maker that toasts four to six sandwiches at a time because it takes quite a few minutes for each one to toast. You may, for example, have four customers at the same table who all order toasted sandwiches. If your machine only toasts two at a time, you will have to try to keep the first two hot while you make the remaining two, in order to serve everyone at the same time.

If you lack space, or you cannot afford to buy a toasted sandwich maker, you can use your panini contact grill to toast sandwiches.

TOASTER

An ordinary toaster is necessary for serving dishes such as scrambled egg or beans on toast. Again I would recommend one that toasts at least four slices at one time. Remember, if you purchase a domestic toaster you will not be given a warranty. A four- slice commercial toaster can cost from approximately £100 up to £250 and you can purchase a six-slice commercial toaster from about £150.

We use a domestic toaster and just replace it when anything goes wrong, but you must consider how much yours is going to be used and then decide what type you think would suit your business..

SOUP KETTLE

A soup kettle is not expensive but in my opinion it is invaluable if you are going to serve home-made soup. It will hold approximately 10 litres of soup, it is thermostatically controlled and it has an inner removable pot for easy cleaning. A soup kettle costs from approximately £70 to £235.

Soup has to be served at a high temperature of 63°C or above. A soup kettle will keep it at the correct temperature and at the same time prevent your soup sticking to the bottom of the pot. If you leave soup simmering on top of the cooker during lunchtime, more than likely it will stick to the bottom of the pot and in some cases burn. Once this happens there is no way you can serve it and it will have to be thrown away.

FOOD MIXER

Don't be tempted to purchase a small domestic food mixer if you are going to be doing all your own baking as it will not last. A good food mixer like a Kenwood Chef or a Kitchen Aid is essential but if you intend to do a lot of baking and you want to splash out you can purchase a Buffalo mixer which will cost you over £1,000.

The cost of a Kitchen Aid mixer is from approximately £234 and a Kenwood Chef from approximately £200.

I do a large amount of baking and I have a Kenwood Chef which cost £352. It has an extra strong gearbox, an 800-watt motor and a 6.7-litre mixing bowl.

LIQUIDIZER OR HAND BLENDER

A liquidizer is handy but I tend to use a hand blender more because I find it is quicker and less expensive than a conventional blender. You could probably buy a good-quality domestic blender or liquidizer as they are relatively inexpensive and you should be able to afford to replace them when they break down.

Commercial liquidizers can cost anything from £100 upwards, as opposed to £20 upwards for a domestic one. You can purchase a domestic hand blender for a few pounds but you can pay from £75 to £200 for a heavy-duty commercial one.

ROBOT COUPE

This is a professional food processor which will grate, slice and chop all your vegetables and also grate your cheese, liquidize soup and make fresh breadcrumbs. It comes with 2 mm and 3 mm slicing and grating discs. The Robot Coupe is expensive but, if you are going to make your own soup, coleslaw and grate your own cheese, this machine is invaluable. You can, however, purchase a domestic food processor but you will not get a commercial warranty with this.

The price of a Robot Coupe is in excess of £500 but you can lease one from £4.55 per week. The website is www.nisbets.com and the telephone number is 0845 1405555.

 **TIP** Should you decide to purchase any domestic items of equipment to use in your coffee shop kitchen, the retailer will not give you any guarantee. Therefore, unless the piece of equipment is inexpensive, and you don't mind replacing it when it stops working, you should always purchase commercial equipment.

FOOD THERMOMETER WITH PROBE

This is another essential piece of equipment because you will have to take the core temperature of any hot food, whether it is freshly cooked or reheated, to make sure that it has reached the correct temperature, 82°C for reheated food and 63°C for holding food hot (see page 103), before you serve it to your customers. You will also have to record the temperature of hot and reheated food twice a day on a temperature control chart.

You can purchase a basic food thermometer from as little as £11.

COLOUR-CODED CHOPPING BOARDS

You will need to purchase chopping boards which are colour-coded so that bacteria are not transferred from one type of food to another. A good chopping board should not split or warp and you should be able to put it through the dishwasher.

- ☐ White is used for bakery and dairy food;

- ☐ Brown is used for vegetables;

- ☐ Green is used for salads and fruit;

- ☐ Blue is used for raw fish;

- ☐ Yellow is used for cooked meat;

- ☐ Red is used for raw meat.

The most economical way to purchase these boards is in a pack which contains one of each colour and a free stand which is approximately £30 including VAT. You can also purchase antibacterial high-density chopping boards which come in the same colours but are a bit more expensive, costing approximately £11.74 each including VAT.

Extra boards can be purchased singly if required.

SINK

You are required by the Environmental Health Department to have a large double sink installed.

WASH HAND BASIN

You have to have at least one wash hand basin installed because you are not allowed to use the sinks to wash your hands. The Environmental Health Officer will require you to supply antibacterial soap in a dispenser and paper towels for each hand sink. Paper towels are more hygienic than cloth towels which can spread bacteria from user to user.

RUBBISH BIN

A rubbish bin with a swing-top lid, conveniently placed in your kitchen, is a good idea as it is a nuisance having to take the lid off the bin every time you put rubbish in it. According to the Environmental Health Officer, you are not allowed to use a rubbish bin without a lid.

Do also put a smaller bin in the coffee shop for customers to put their rubbish in otherwise they will leave it on the table or drop it on the floor for your staff to pick up.

 Use a black bin liner as it keeps the bin cleaner and ask your staff to wash out the bin with disinfectant every night.

We have a Biffa Bin, which is a bin for commercial waste, placed outside at the back of the coffee shop and it is emptied every week. It would surprise you just how much is thrown away, especially empty drinks cans. If you find you have a lot of waste it would be worthwhile making enquiries from your local council about a Biffa Bin. There is a charge for emptying it.

MAGNETIC STRIP FOR KNIVES

You can put all your knives onto this strong magnetic strip, which makes it easier and quicker to choose the knife you want to use and also prevents blade damage. These are relatively cheap to buy, costing approximately £11 each including VAT.

ORDER STRIP

This is a strip which is fixed to the wall in the kitchen so that orders taken can be put directly onto it in the sequence in which the order is taken. This lets you see at a glance what orders have come into the kitchen, and if more than one person is preparing food, everyone knows which has to be prepared first.

FLY-KILLER

These are necessary for your kitchen and for the sitting area in your coffee shop. They are electrical units which are fixed to the wall or ceiling. They have a drawer beneath them which traps flies and insects. The drawer should be emptied of dead insects on a regular basis. They are supplied either wall- or ceiling-mounted and are available in various sizes. They cost from around £35.

OTHER KITCHEN EQUIPMENT YOU WILL NEED

Good heavy pots and a frying pan (you require a heavy base so that you don't burn soup when you are making it);

- A colander;

- Sieves;

- A good set of knives, including vegetable knife, bread knife, carving knife, chopping knife, palette knife;

- Whisks;

- Potato peelers;

- Wooden spoons;

- Slotted spoons;

- Large serving spoons;

- Tongs;

- Measuring spoons;

- Spatulas;

- Ladles;

- Kitchen scissors;

☐ Food scales (digital are better because they are more accurate for measuring small quantities);

☐ Baking trays (a few different sizes);

☐ Pastry brushes;

☐ Lemon zester;

☐ Mixing bowls (a few different sizes);

☐ Measuring jug;

☐ Plastic food storage containers.

TABLEWARE

White, rather than patterned, tableware is best. Food looks better on it and it's easier to replace. Try to get hardwearing tableware which is oven, microwave, dishwasher and freezer proof. You would be surprised how much crockery gets chipped and broken

You will need the following:

☐ Soup bowls;

☐ Tea plates;

☐ Medium-sized dinner plates;

☐ Large dinner plates (if you decide to increase your menu to include light meals);

☐ Salt and pepper pots (try to get containers that don't need to be filled every five minutes and that have good-fitting tops);

 Do get your staff to check the salt and pepper pots each night to ensure that the tops are tightly closed because some children loosen them for a joke.

We have had to replace a few meals because a child has loosened the top of one of the salt or pepper pots. Of course, when the next customer has used it, the whole pot has emptied over their meal.

☐ Small stainless steel milk jugs (this works out cheaper than supplying individual portions of milk);

☐ Large sugar dispensers for each table. They can be glass or plastic so that you staff can see when they need to be refilled. Free pour dispensers are best;

- ☐ Tumblers (for cold drinks) that can be chilled without breaking;

- ☐ Teapots for one and two people;

- ☐ Teacups and saucers;

- ☐ Tall café latte glasses for speciality coffees;

- ☐ Espresso cups and saucers;

- ☐ Cappuccino cups and saucers.

If you are going to offer two or three sizes of coffee you will have to purchase different-sized coffee cups and mugs.

Do make sure you get heavy-duty coffee mugs and cappuccino cups and saucers that won't break or chip easily. However, they must be inexpensive enough for you to be able to replace them when they get broken by your staff or customers.

A few coffee suppliers will supply you with mugs, espresso cups and saucers and cappuccino cups and saucers if you agree to purchase all your coffee from them. Ask the representative of your coffee supplier what perks they can offer you.

CUTLERY

Good-quality plain stainless steel cutlery is best because it won't date, it will last longer and you can replace it easily.

- ☐ Knives;

- ☐ Forks;

- ☐ Soup spoons;

- ☐ Teaspoons.

It is surprising how many customers will just take your teaspoons home with them, and also how many will be thrown out by accident by your staff. If you find you are losing a lot of teaspoons you can buy plastic stirrers. My view is that plastic stirrers look tatty and although we lose about 100 teaspoons every year we still prefer them to the plastic disposable alternatives.

Purchase the least expensive teaspoons you can find.

NAPKIN DISPENSERS

Despite the cost, it is advisable to purchase a napkin dispenser because it cuts down the number of napkins a customer will take at one time.

You might want to place a sign beside the napkin dispenser asking your customers to take only the number of napkins they need.

CASH REGISTER

There are many different styles of cash register on the market and your choice depends on what you need it to do for you. We recently replaced our basic cash register with a sophisticated one which can tell you at the push of a button:

☐ how much money you take in a day, in any number of weeks, or in a year;

☐ the average spend per customer;

☐ how many of a particular item were sold in a day, in any number of weeks, or in a year.

This allows us to know which items are our best sellers and which are poor sellers, and other important sales information.

It is not necessary to have such a sophisticated cash register so do your homework and find one that will do everything you want it to do and will last you for a long time because they are not cheap. You can buy a simple cash register for about £100 but you could probably purchase a second-hand one for a fraction of the price.

If you want to purchase, lease or just find out the price of items of equipment for your kitchen, look at the website for Nisbets who offer a quick delivery service for most items. They also offer a leasing service for some equipment. The website is www.nisbets.com and the telephone number is 0845 1405555. Also check your Yellow Pages and the internet for other suppliers as it is always better to shop around for the best price.

Buying furniture and fittings
TABLES

Do purchase tables that are easy to clean, whether they are made of wood, glass or Formica. If you decide to have tablecloths, remember that you will either have to wash them yourself each night or you will have to send them to the laundry, unless they are made from oilcloth and then you can just wipe them clean.

A coffee shop owner once informed me that if you send tablecloths to the laundry and submit this account against your income tax return, then the Inland Revenue can calculate how many tables you serve in the year. I'm not sure whether to believe this tale or not!

> *I knew someone who thought that marble tables would look great in his restaurant. Unfortunately though they stained easily and some of the stains were impossible to remove.*

Consider having tables that seat two or four people; if you have a larger party you can always put two tables together. You will find that your customers are usually made up of two people or a family of four. Please don't put the tables too close together as people like some space and don't want to think that their neighbours are listening to everything they say.

CHAIRS

A comfortable chair is essential so choose the chairs for your coffee shop with care. Avoid straight, high-back chairs, bar stools and chairs that are very low and difficult to get out of. These are all very uncomfortable. Basket chairs and benches with padded cushions are relatively comfortable.

Before you make a purchase try out several chairs to see what you think is the most comfortable one. If you wouldn't like to sit on a chair for a period of time, neither will your customers.

Choose chairs that are well made and strong because you will find that customers will rock backwards and forwards on their chairs and you don't want to be sued if one collapses when someone is seated.

If you have sufficient space, it is prudent to keep a few extra chairs so that you can immediately replace any that become damaged or broken. Customers are not always careful with your furniture and they often allow their children to climb and stand on the chairs. In the current litigious culture customers could well try to sue you for damages if they are injured because of a broken or damaged chair.

HIGH CHAIRS

Do buy at least two high chairs because they are essential if you are going to be a child-friendly coffee shop and want to encourage parents and grandparents to come into your shop with their youngsters.

7
CHOOSING YOUR SUPPLIERS

Once you have decided what products you require, your next step is to choose suppliers for these products. If you can do this before you open, you will save valuable time that would be spent later, searching through the Yellow Pages and the internet. Ask other coffee shop or restaurant owners for advice in choosing suppliers because they will know, through experience, which ones to use and which ones to avoid.

Finding your food suppliers

Do make a list of what products you are going to require and then choose suppliers for these products. You will find out very quickly that you won't be able to obtain everything you need from one supplier.

Here are some of the suppliers you will require:

☐ **Baker** for fresh bread, rolls, croissants and cakes

☐ **Greengrocer** for fresh fruit and vegetables
You will require fresh vegetables for making soup and fresh salad ingredients for salad garnish and salads.

☐ **Milkman** for milk and cream
Full cream milk is necessary for making cappuccinos and you will require cream for cake fillings, making cheesecakes and to serve with apple pies etc.

☐ **Butcher** for ham, bacon, sausages, burgers and cold meats

☐ **Coffee beans and flavoured syrups** can be supplied by the company from which you lease or purchase your coffee machine.

☐ **Baking ingredients** can be purchased from a specialist company, e.g. Bako, or from the supermarket. However, you could check with your general supplier who may be able to supply you with these products.

☐ **General supplier** for frozen foods, including paninis, and run of the mill things like cheese, bacon, mayonnaise, sugar, salt, jam and butter portions and much more.

☐ You can also get a special oven on loan as long as you agree to purchase paninis and pastries from a well-known company but I think it is a very expensive way of providing this type of food.

☐ **Newsagent** – have a newsagent deliver daily papers and a few magazines for your customers to read while they are enjoying a coffee and cake in your shop.

 **TIP** I find that frozen paninis are much better for our coffee shop because they can be taken out of the freezer in the morning and defrosted ready to use from mid morning. If you run out of defrosted paninis you can put them in the microwave and they will defrost in a few minutes.

As I mentioned previously, you can find suppliers' names from asking other coffee shop or restaurant owners or by looking through your local Yellow Pages. Don't be afraid to ask other coffee shop owners where they buy their fruit and vegetables, bread, cakes, etc. If they don't want to give you this information they can always say no.

I asked a coffee shop owner from another town who he bought his produce from and he was good enough to give me a list of his suppliers. This was a great help to me and it does show that some people are only too willing to help someone new to the business.

Take into account the suppliers' reputation, the quality and price of their products, their delivery times and reliability. You don't want to be still waiting for your fresh milk, morning rolls and bread to be delivered after opening time.

ESTABLISHING A RAPPORT WITH YOUR SUPPLIERS

It is important to establish a good relationship with your suppliers because they can be very helpful. For example, if you forget to order a product and they have a few extra on their delivery van they will usually give them to you to help you out. They will also know what products sell well and can recommend that you try them out, or they may even give you a few free samples to try.

Ask a sales representative to meet you to discuss their company's terms and conditions. You may also want to ask some of the following:

☐ Can they give you a printout of the products they can supply and the prices they are going to charge you for them? You can compare price lists with those of other companies.

☐ Do they give discount for larger orders?

☐ How often do they deliver to your area?

☐ What time of day will they deliver to your shop?

☐ What time does the order have to be telephoned in to them for next-day delivery?

☐ Do they have an answering machine for taking orders out of business hours?

> *Occasionally I have remembered an item I had forgotten to order during the day and I have left a message on the answering machine after midnight for the order to be delivered the following day.*

Will they give you the names and contact numbers of a few of their other customers so that you can get a reference from them? Suppliers are usually keen to do business with you and if they have nothing to hide they will be only too glad to give you this information.

Always be polite to the sales reps on the phone, and when they visit your coffee shop you could offer them a cup of coffee while you discuss business with them. This will help build up a good relationship with the supplier.

 If you can obtain a product from another supplier at a cheaper price, inform the representative of your normal supplier and they will usually agree to reduce their price or match the other supplier's price.

ASKING FOR CREDIT

Initially you won't get credit from suppliers until you make an application for credit and you are able to supply them with trade references. If you are starting a new business, more than likely you won't have any credit references and in that case the suppliers usually like you to pay cash on delivery for a certain period of time. Once you have done this for the time specified you should then be able to apply for credit. Having credit accounts will give you time to pay your bills but make sure you pay your suppliers on time as they also need to pay their bills.

 **If you don't have any trade references, ask your suppliers if you can use personal credit references including a reference from your bank. If they won't allow this then you should respect their decision because they are only protecting themselves against bad debts.**

Do type out a list of products so that you can use this list each time you place an order. For example, you can put a number or a tick beside each item you require and, when you telephone your order, you just have to read it off the list. Some suppliers have ordering forms you can use and if this is the case ask them for a good supply or photocopy a good amount for yourself.

Make sure that you state clearly when you telephone your order whether you require one case or one box as a case consists of a number of boxes.

Some orders you will have to get daily, and probably before you open in the morning, for example, milk, bread, rolls and fresh vegetables. If you are buying in cakes, scones and tray bakes, you will also have to have these delivered before you open for business.

We don't have a lot of freezer space so we usually get our frozen products delivered as we need them. The benefit of this is that our frozen products are down to the last few before we replace them.

We are very lucky in that our main supplier delivers six days a week.

Ask the baker who is supplying your rolls and bread to give you samples of other special breads and rolls. This way you can try various different types before you decide to place an order for any of them. The baker should also give you samples of cakes if you are not going to bake your own.

Try to get other orders delivered at a time when the coffee shop is quieter so as not to disrupt business. You will also want to put away the food immediately, especially if you have some frozen and refrigerated items in your delivery.

CHECKING YOUR ORDER

When your order arrives, always check it carefully, no matter how busy you are, to verify that everything you ordered has arrived. Tick items off the delivery note before you sign it because if the delivery person is in a hurry, they could leave something on the van in error.

Do always check the use by dates on each item and if anything is unacceptable in terms of quality, out of date, has a short lifespan, or is partially defrosted, then send it back at the time of delivery. Mark clearly on the delivery note why it is being returned and ask for a replacement. Once you have signed the delivery note you have accepted the order and it would be very difficult then to go back and complain to the supplier.

Never be tempted to use inferior produce because you think it is too much trouble to send it back, or because you don't want to upset your supplier.

If you are not satisfied with the freshness of the produce you receive, you can always change suppliers. However, most suppliers are keen to keep your business and they are very careful about what they deliver.

Buying from supermarkets

Sometimes it is cheaper and more convenient to purchase some of your stock from a supermarket.

☐ You don't have to buy in large amounts or large packages or jars;

☐ You can place your order online in the evening to save time at work;

☐ You can have it delivered for a small charge, or free if you place a large order;

☐ You can purchase more unusual items;

☐ The produce is usually fresh.

When we first opened our coffee shop we bought almost everything from a local supermarket because we did not know the quantities we would use, and for us this was the best way. I would go to the supermarket in the morning before opening the coffee shop and get what I thought we required for the day. This, however, was time-consuming and expensive so, over time, I gradually ordered most of the goods from suppliers and settled for a single order delivered from the supermarket once a week.

Using a cash and carry

If you have a 'cash and carry' outlet in your area do go and look around and compare prices and products. They are handy if your supplier has run out of a product you require immediately. Sometimes too they have more unusual products which you may like to try out.

The downside of using a cash and carry is the time it takes out of your day or evening. Remember, you will have to walk around the various aisles choosing products and then, after you have paid for them, you have to load up your car. You are not finished even then because you have to unload the goods at the coffee shop and put everything away in its place.

You will probably have to buy in bulk; for example, a case of baked beans or a case of mayonnaise. If you don't have the storage space, or if you are not going to be able to use the whole case before the use by date, don't be tempted to buy this way.

The benefit of most cash and carry units is that they are usually open from early in the morning until late at night. Despite this, I would recommend that, if you are going to use the cash and carry, you try to use it only once a week.

Handling food safely

FROZEN FOOD

Put frozen products away first, placing them beneath older items in your freezer, because you need to rotate your stock and use the food in date order. Stock rotation is important, not only to maintain quality and freshness, but also because of waste. You don't want to have to throw away products that have been buried for months under newer stock and then you find they are out of date.

 If you are getting a delivery from the butcher, ask them to put labels with the date onto each item before it is delivered to you.

REFRIGERATED FOOD

Next, put your refrigerated products away and again move the older items to the front of the fridge with use by dates visible so that they are easily seen by the staff.

BREAD

If you are going to store bread, to retain freshness it must always be frozen immediately and not kept in the fridge.

 Try to have your bread and rolls delivered daily, especially when you are using them for sandwiches. If you have to use bread that has been frozen it is best used for toasted sandwiches and toast.

CANS AND DRIED FOODS

Store these in dry cupboards, and remember to rotate your stock with the earliest sell by date at the front of the shelves. Put your drink cans into the chiller cabinet and again remember to rotate your stock.

 Once a can of food has been opened, never put the contents into the fridge still in the can; always empty the contents into a clean container, cover, and then put into the fridge.

8
EMPLOYING STAFF

It is very important to choose your staff with care. Ideally, you want to employ someone who is going to be an asset to your business. You want staff who will smile and be friendly towards customers, and who are honest and reliable. If you find someone good you can train them to be great.

Once you have found your ideal recruit you are obliged to provide them with an employment contract. It is likely that your staff will be employed on a full-time or part-time basis – I have included in Appendices 1-3 examples of employment contracts for:

☐ full-time staff;

☐ part-time staff;

☐ part-time (weekend) staff.

These contract documents reflect what I use in my coffee shop. You will of course have to tailor them to meet your own unique requirements.

Deciding how many staff you need

You will simply not be able to do everything yourself and you will have to consider employing someone to help you. You can begin by getting one full-time person and one or two part-time workers. The part-time workers may be interested in working full time when the need arises but in the meantime you will know how many workers you will require to work certain hours during the day, e.g. during lunchtime between 12 noon and 2 p.m.

Do not employ too many staff to begin with because it will be very difficult to terminate someone's employment if you find that business is slow. Only when your coffee shop gets busier should you think about employing other workers.

 If you employ a worker part-time and their wage is under £100 per week they will not have to pay income tax or national insurance contributions.

Employing immigrants

More people are coming from Europe to seek work in the UK. If you are considering employing one of these people, you need to ensure that he or she has the right to work here.

All citizens of the European Union have the right to come to the UK but not all of them necessarily have the right to work in the UK! You should check the applicant's documents before the person starts work. If the person has the right to work in the UK, they will be able to produce the following documents:

☐ a passport confirming that the applicant is a British citizen;

☐ a document giving the applicant's National Insurance number, plus their full UK birth certificate;

☐ a passport or identity card of an EEA (European Economic Area) national.

If the applicant is from Romania or Bulgaria they will require more evidence of their right to work.

Since January 2007, when Romania and Bulgaria joined the EU, people from these two countries have been allowed to come into the UK without visas but they are not permitted to work in the UK without a Work Authorization Document. Similar restrictions apply to non-EU immigrants.

It is a criminal offence to employ anyone who is not entitled to work in the UK. Therefore, it is essential that you ensure that the person you are considering employing has the right to work in this country.

There is a penalty of £5,000 for each person you employ who is an unregistered worker from any of the following countries:

Latvia, Slovakia, Poland, Czech Republic, Lithuania, Slovenia, Estonia and Hungary.

If you employ a worker from any of these countries you must make sure they have the right to work in this country by checking their EEA (European Economic Area) passport or identity card. You must then advise the worker to complete an application form and send it, along with evidence of their employment, to the Home Office to register immediately they start work.

If you are considering employing someone from Europe, do contact the Home Office to get up-to-date information on recruitment and immigration. A list of acceptable documents to confirm the right to work in the UK is available from the Home Office website, www.homeoffice.gov.uk or, for more information, you can ring the Home Office Employers' Helpline on 0845 010 6677.

Recruiting your staff

Finding the right staff is very important because they represent your business. Good staff can help you to create a warm, welcoming atmosphere in your coffee shop. Poor staff on the other hand can scare away your customers. So give yourself plenty of time to find staff before you open your coffee shop.

ADVERTISING IN YOUR LOCAL NEWSPAPER

Placing an advert in your local newspaper is a good way of finding staff because all jobseekers read the vacancy pages in their newspaper. Also you tend to attract local people who don't have to travel far to their employment. This is an advantage if you require staff to work at short notice – for instance, if another member of staff has telephoned in sick.

The wording of your advertisement is crucial in attracting the right person for the job, so make sure you get it right.

Some things to consider when writing a job advertisement

☐ Keep it short and simple (you will be charged by the line);

☐ Give the name and address of your coffee shop and include your logo if you have one;

☐ State the job title and the type of person you are looking for, e.g. experienced, friendly, outgoing;

☐ State the hours required and if you want the employee to cover holidays, sickness, etc.;

☐ Give the starting date;

☐ Include details on how to reply and to whom and the closing date for applications.

Although you are trying to keep your advertisement short, try to make it interesting enough so that if you were to read it yourself, you would be tempted to apply for the job.

ADVERTISING IN YOUR OWN SHOP

This is an inexpensive way of finding staff. You could display a notice inside the shop and another on the window asking people to apply for the position. You will be able to customize your own application form and ask all people who are interested in the job to complete one. You will want them to answer specific questions which should include the names and contact numbers of referees.

Always check the references of anyone you are considering for a job because you would be surprised how many people lie about their previous employment.

> *I interviewed a potential member of staff who informed me that he had baked all the cakes, tray bakes and gateaux in his previous employment. However, when I checked with the owner of that particular coffee shop, I was informed that he had never heard of the person and he had certainly not been employed there.*

USING THE JOB CENTRE

This is a free national service and it is underused by companies. Sometimes you can be lucky and get a really good, experienced candidate through this service. However, I have discovered that the majority of applications you get are from candidates who don't fit your profile. Do ask the person taking details of the vacancy from you not to give application forms to anyone who does not fulfil the criteria you have set. Quite often the Job Centre will give application forms to people who are not really interested in your job but they must make applications or attend interviews in order to continue to qualify for benefits. Often they don't turn up for an interview if you do contact them.

CONTACTING YOU LOCAL COLLEGE

You could contact your local college and ask the catering department if they know anyone suitable who might be interested in a job in your shop. If they don't know anyone at that time, type out an interesting advert, send it to the college and ask if they would display it on the college notice board.

USING AN AGENCY

Don't contact an agency unless you are really desperate as this can be a very costly way of finding staff.

> *We nearly employed a young man who was recommended by an agency. Before we did so, we checked his references from his previous employer and discovered that he had been given the sack because he allegedly put cannabis into the lasagne he was making. I was surprised that the agency hadn't checked his references before taking him on as a client.*

WORD OF MOUTH

Once your coffee shop has opened you can often attract good staff by word of mouth via friends and customers. However, it is not always a good thing to employ a friend of a friend because if things don't work out it can be awkward.

THE NEW DEAL SCHEME

New Deal is a key part of the Government's Welfare to Work strategy. It aims to give unemployed people new opportunities to train and gain work experience, and to help businesses that have staff shortages.

Everyone taking part in New Deal has a personal adviser who provides support and arranges training, if required, before the person is ready to be employed. By the time the candidate is presented to you they should be employable because they have been through a skills assessment and, where necessary, given training to update their skills to prepare them for work. Support is provided to the employer after the person has started work.

Financial help is also given to the employer through an employment subsidy which is paid for 26 weeks.

New Deal Plus

This is for people aged 25 and over who have been unemployed for at least six months. You receive:

☐ £75 a week for each person employed by you for at least 30 hours per week;

☐ £50 a week for each person employed by you between 16 to 29 hours per week.

New Deal for Young People

This is for people aged 16 to 25. If you take on anyone under New Deal for Young People, you can get a grant of up to £750 towards the cost of an agreed qualification or training certificate. You can train them in your business or you can send them to college. You receive:

☐ £60 a week for each person employed by you for at least 30 hours per week;

☐ £40 a week for each person employed by you for 24 to 29 hours per week.

You will be asked to sign an agreement confirming that you will:

☐ keep the person for as long as they show the ability and commitment you need;

☐ give them the same training as anyone else doing the job;

☐ monitor and record their progress and identify the areas for action, in the same way you would for any other employee, to help them settle in and make progress;

☐ employ them for at least 26 weeks;

☐ fill in a health and safety questionnaire to ensure that your business meets certain standards.

For more information or to place a vacancy you can contact the Job Centre Plus on www.jobcentreplus.gov.uk/employers or telephone 0845 601 2001.

WORK TRIALS

Work trials allow you to find out if a person is suited to the job you are offering and it also lets the person see if it is the right job for them.

A person has to have been out of work for at least six months. They will continue to receive benefit, travel expenses and a meal allowance while they are on trial.

Again you will have to sign an agreement and fill in a health and safety questionnaire.

You will have to employ the person for 16 or more hours per week.

For more information or to place a vacancy you can contact the Job Centre Plus on www.jobcentreplus.gov.uk/employers or telephone 0845 601 2001.

BACK TO WORK

There is a Government-funded scheme to help support people back into work who have been out of work for a set period of time. The programme gives them an opportunity to gain work experience and training.

You are required to offer the worker an opportunity to gain experience in the workplace and they are paid by the government so they have an incentive to work. They are technically supposed to be surplus to the core workforce and they will be paid by the government for 20 hours a week for six months.

You can assess the worker over the six-month period with a view to employing them yourself on a permanent basis, or you can apply for another worker through the scheme. During the six-month period you can part company with the worker if you think they are not suitable for your business. Before you take part in this scheme your business will have to be assessed against a health and safety checklist and you will have to agree to some basic requirements.

To enquire about obtaining staff through a Government-funded scheme, contact your local Job Centre Plus or Employer Direct. They will get a labour market adviser to contact you with the information available for the type of person you wish to employ. You can get in touch with Employer Direct from Monday to Friday, 8 a.m. until 8 p.m. and Saturday, 10 a.m. until 4 p.m. The telephone number is 0845 601 2001.

SKILLSEEKERS

Skillseekers is only available in Scotland and the training is funded by the government.

The employer has to pay the Skillseeker an allowance of a minimum of £55 per week (it is up to the employer if they want to pay more) and the Government funds the training. The Skillseeker usually works four days a week and spends one day a week at a college or approved training supplier who will provide and manage the training.

To talk through options and find out more, contact the Careers Scotland Centre on 0845 8502502; your local Enterprise Agency; or Skills Development Scotland, 150 Broomielaw, Atlantic Quay, Glasgow, G2 8LU. Their website is www.skillsdevelopmentscotland.co.uk and their email address is info@skillsdevelopment.co.uk

In England the Modern Apprenticeship is a similar scheme. It is up to the employer what they pay the employee and there is no minimum allowance. Again the training is

Government-funded and the employee is expected to work four days a week and attend college for training one day a week.

For further information and advice telephone 08000 150 400 or check out the website, www.employersforapprenticeships.gov.uk

The Learning and Skills Council find and manage apprenticeships in England. Their website is www.apprenticeships.org.uk

STUDENTS

Students are usually interested in earning extra pocket money but they are only available at weekends or during school, college or university holidays. They are generally good workers and you can find them by contacting local schools, colleges and universities and asking them to display an advertisement on their notice board.

The downside of employing a student is that they are often out late on a Friday night with their friends and there is a chance that they will phone in sick on a Saturday morning. This of course is the time you need them most.

Interviewing prospective employees

The interview is your opportunity to assess each candidate carefully and make sure you pick the right person for the job. It can be a daunting task so it essential to prepare well in advance.

DEFINING THE JOB

Before the interview you should prepare a job description form and show this to the candidate. It should be succinct and cover the key features of the job. (I have included a one-page pro forma in Appendix 4.)

When you have made a job offer, and the candidate has accepted this, they should sign the form to say that they have read it and agree to carry out the duties detailed on it. You should then give them a copy and keep a copy on file. You can refer to this if, in the future, the member of staff complains that 'That's not my job'.

PREPARING YOUR QUESTIONS

It is essential to prepare a list of questions that you want to ask candidates at interview so that you keep the discussions on track. Don't be tempted to make up the questions as you go along as you won't find out the details you really want to know. Print out your list of questions and leave enough room on the paper to make concise notes during the interview. Don't try to write down everything that is said; you won't be able to concentrate on the interview. Wait until after the interview, then write down your impressions while they are still fresh in your mind. Leave at least 15 minutes between interviews to allow you to complete your notes for each candidate.

At the end of each interview staple the interview questionnaire to the job application or Curriculum Vitae so that you have all the information to hand about each candidate when you come to make your decision.

CONDUCTING THE INTERVIEW

Ask the applicants to come for an interview at a specific time, and allow half an hour for each appointment. Set aside a period of time, say 4 p.m. to 6 p.m. on a quiet day, so that you are not rushed. Set up the interview in a comfortable place and try to create a relaxed atmosphere to allow the candidates to feel at ease. Do your best to ensure that you are not interrupted during the interviews, either by the telephone ringing or by other members of staff.

You should begin the interview by telling the applicant a bit about your business and describing the duties involved in the job, the working hours and the wages. Point out any perks that go with the job – for example, how the tips are divided, any discount on food and drink in the coffee shop, or a free lunch during working hours.

The questions you ask should be designed to find out if candidates have the skills and qualities required for the job, so use open questions – those that begin with the words how, why, where, when, what, etc. – to encourage candidates to talk.

As well as asking the right questions, you need to have good listening skills so that you are able to interpret what is being said and, if necessary, tease out anything you feel is being withheld.

Summarize from time to time during the interview, to clarify what information you have obtained, and then move on to another topic.

Questions you should ask

☐ Do they have any relevant work experience and what do they think they can bring to the job?

☐ What do they think their strengths and weaknesses are?

☐ What did they enjoy most about their previous job?

☐ How do they react to criticism?

☐ How did they get on with their previous employer?

☐ What was their reason for leaving their previous job? (If aspects of their previous job that they didn't like are present in the job you are offering, this will cause problems – for example, if someone didn't like being told what to do, or they didn't like having to work at weekends, you are certainly going to have problems.)

 Something which I found useful was to ask the candidate what they would do in a particular scenario, for example, if a customer complained that his coffee wasn't served hot enough, or he was given the wrong filling in his sandwich.

How many days have they had off work for sickness in the last two years? (You don't want to employ someone who is in the habit of taking days off on a regular basis.)

What do they expect from the job?

At the end of the interview ask the candidate if there are any questions they would like to ask you about the job. Remember to enquire if they have any holidays booked, when they can start working for you and, if they are presently working, what notice they have to give their employers.

You should ask if they have any doubts about this position and if they still wish to be considered for it now that they have heard what is expected of them.

> *Someone I know always drops a piece of paper on the floor when he is showing a candidate into the room for their interview, to see if they pick it up. He maintains that it says a lot about whether a person is tidy or not.*

Questions you are not allowed to ask
It is illegal to discriminate on grounds of:

Race
☐ You cannot ask questions on ethnic background or country of origin.

Sex
☐ You cannot ask someone if they are planning to start a family and then use an affirmative answer as a reason for not employing them.

Disability
☐ You cannot use a person's disability as a reason not to employ them unless you can justify this.

Dismissing staff
This can be one of your most difficult tasks. It is somewhat unfair, and an oversimplification, to suggest that you can avoid the necessity of dismissing an employee if you take care in selecting your staff in the first place, and in training, cajoling and guiding them thereafter. Occasionally you may have a member of staff who is either just not capable of discharging their tasks or through stubbornness believes that your rules are for others and not for themselves.

Running a coffee shop with a very small staff may not be in the same league as running a large manufacturing organization with thousands of employees but the relationship between you and your staff is essentially the same.

Should the situation arise when you feel that staff behaviour has crossed the line such that you have no alternative but to dismiss the employee, then it is essential that you follow the statutory disciplinary and dismissal procedure (DDPs) in precisely the same way as the manager of the large manufacturing organization would.

You and your staff will deal directly with the public and you have a duty of care for the public's safety and health. So the responsibilities of your staff must not be trivialized and should they fall short then you must take appropriate action.

You must know what to do before the situation arises – you will not have time to read the literature once you are faced with a volatile situation that could lead to a dismissal.

The Employment Act (Dispute Resolution) is updated from time to time so it is useful to familiarize yourself with the up-to-date advice on resolving disputes from the Department of Trade and Industry: see www.dti.gov.uk/er/resolvingdisputes.htm

There is plenty of literature to help you. The text which follows is a fairly loose extraction from some of this freely available literature and as such forms a summary of the main rules which you must follow. There is also an excellent and fairly succinct fact sheet by Cobweb Information Ltd which is available from www.scavenger.net for a small fee.

WHEN YOU MAY DISMISS AN EMPLOYEE

You may dismiss an employee for:

- ☐ misconduct;

- ☐ inability to perform;

- ☐ redundancy;

- ☐ other substantial reasons.

Misconduct

Dismissing an employee for misconduct is usually the most straightforward of all dismissal situations – but only if you have prepared the way by having the necessary rules in place for your business.

Write down clear, reasonable rules and procedures. They should include:

- ☐ an explanation of which are disciplinary offences;

- ☐ what procedures will be followed if an employee commits a disciplinary offence, (these procedures must now be at least as good as the statutory minimum);

- ☐ which offences provide grounds for summary dismissal;

- ☐ what rights of representation and appeal the employees have.

Make employees aware of the rules.

☐ Give each employee a copy of the rules and explain them. It is difficult to discipline employees for breaking rules they are not aware of.

☐ You are legally required either to include the rules and procedures in your written terms of employment or to make it plain where a copy is available.

Most offences will lead to a series of oral and written warnings before any dismissal.

☐ Investigate the circumstances of the offence before taking any formal action.

☐ Typically, you might give an employee one spoken warning and two written warnings before dismissal. Spoken warnings will often be removed from an employee's disciplinary record after six months, and written warnings after 12 months (if there are no further disciplinary offences).

☐ A formal warning should include a time limit within which you expect improvement, and an explanation of the consequences otherwise.

☐ Apply the rules fairly and consistently. An employee who can show that you applied the rules inconsistently may be able to claim unfair dismissal.

☐ Keep written records of all disciplinary action you take. Include a record of any steps you have taken to investigate and address the cause of the problem.

☐ All employees have the right to be accompanied by a colleague or trade union official at any disciplinary hearing.

☐ Remind employees of their right to explain their conduct or suggest counter-proposals.

'Gross misconduct' can provide grounds for summary dismissal, but the statutory procedure must still be followed.

☐ Gross misconduct typically includes theft, fighting or physical assault, drunkenness or drug-taking, wilful damage to company property, and intentional or reckless disregard for safety rules.

☐ In most cases the standard procedure involves three steps which must be followed: a written explanation of the problem, a face-to-face meeting, and an opportunity for the employee to appeal.

☐ In exceptional circumstances, you might be justified in using a 'modified', two-step procedure – a written explanation of the problem, with details of why you think the employee is the guilty party, and an opportunity for them to appeal.

Employees have the right to appeal against all disciplinary decisions, including dismissal. Give employees the appropriate notice, unless they have been summarily dismissed.

You must provide written reasons for the dismissal. You are legally required to do this:

□ within 14 days of a written request from an employee who has completed at least one year's continuous employment;

□ whenever you dismiss an employee who is pregnant or on maternity leave, and regardless of how long she has worked for you.

Inability to perform

It is most unlikely that you should need to dismiss someone in your coffee shop for this reason. If you fail to identify such a problem with a candidate at interview, then normally anyone who is incompetent will be discovered fairly soon thereafter. They can then be dismissed without running such a high risk of a claim for unfair dismissal.

There are four 'permitted' reasons for dismissing employees who are unable to perform their jobs, though presumably only the first two will apply to your coffee shop worker:

□ Incompetence (lacking the skills or aptitude to carry out duties effectively);

□ Sickness or injury (usually associated with frequent or prolonged absenteeism, although a long-term sickness or injury may qualify as a disability);

□ Lack of relevant academic, technical or professional qualifications;

□ Because it would be illegal for the employee to carry on working in the job (for example, if the employee loses the required driving licence).

You must be able to demonstrate that you acted fairly and reasonably, both in deciding to dismiss and in the way you did it.

□ Was the employee really unable to perform or was this an excuse for dismissal? For example, has the employee worked satisfactorily in the past?

□ Did you (where needed) provide appropriate support or training?

□ Did you investigate the circumstances fully?

□ Did you consider alternative options?

□ Did you set out your concerns in writing, give the employee time to consider them, then discuss them with the employee?

□ Did you ensure that the employee knew about his or her right to appeal?

Redundancy

You may dismiss an employee because their job has become redundant; if, for example, you downsize your shop.

Other reasons

You may dismiss a member of staff for 'some other substantial reason'; for example, a refusal to co-operate with a generally accepted change in working practices. You may also dismiss a temporary replacement once the permanent employee returns to work (e.g. after maternity leave).

WHEN IT IS UNFAIR OR UNLAWFUL TO DISMISS AN EMPLOYEE

There are a number of reasons for which it will be deemed unfair or indeed unlawful to dismiss an employee.

It is an inadmissible reason to dismiss any employee for:

☐ being pregnant, giving birth or taking advantage of statutory maternity rights;

☐ pointing out or reacting to imminent risks to health and safety;

☐ membership (or non-membership) of a trade union;

☐ questioning or challenging your apparent disregard for statutory employment rights;

☐ reporting superiors or colleagues for illegal or dangerous activities ('whistleblowing');

☐ jury service;

☐ to facilitate the sale of your business.

It is unlawful to dismiss any employee on the grounds of:

☐ sex or marital status;

☐ race, nationality or national or ethnic origins;

☐ sexual orientation, actual or perceived;

☐ disability;

☐ religion or philosophical belief.

Some employers assume that if their employees have not been employed by them for 12 months, they can terminate their employment without being sued for unfair dismissal. That assumption is only partly right and it is risky to rely on it.

Some dismissals are classed as 'automatically unfair', even if the employer acted reasonably at the time of the dismissal and there is no length of service issue. If the employer dismisses an employee for one of these reasons that employee has the right to bring a claim against the employer. There are quite a number of reasons deemed as 'automatically unfair' and I have listed only a few of them below. It is always wise to check out the most up-to-date law. The reasons include:

☐ pregnancy or any reason connected with maternity;

❑ taking, or seeking to take, parental leave, paternity leave, adoption leave or time off for dependants;

❑ failure to return from maternity leave or adoption leave because the employer did not give any, or gave inadequate, notice of when the leave period should end;

❑ refusing or proposing to refuse to do shop work on a Sunday;

❑ grounds relating to the national minimum wage;

❑ grounds relating to Working Tax Credit;

❑ grounds relating to jury service.

If an employee can show that their dismissal was discriminatory under any of the relevant discrimination acts then they can sue their employer for unfair dismissal even though they have not been in continuous employment for 12 months. In this case the compensation claim can be increased as a result of the employer's failure to follow the statutory dismissal procedure.

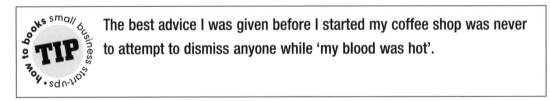

The best advice I was given before I started my coffee shop was never to attempt to dismiss anyone while 'my blood was hot'.

Even in circumstances where the employee's behaviour is clearly gross misconduct and lays them open to immediate dismissal, this should still not be done without following the formal procedure and without carrying out an investigation into the incident in question. It would be best to suspend the employee (on full pay) while an investigation takes place and invite them in writing to attend a formal hearing, prior to making a decision. Don't forget that all employees have the right to appeal.

Don't make hasty decisions

Even at this meeting you should not inform the employee of your intent to dismiss them. This is because a very quick decision may make it look as if you had made up your mind before hearing their side of the story. It is always best to take 24 hours after the final meeting to go over the information that you have, and any additional information that has been supplied by the employee in the meeting, before you make a decision.

The other advice I was given was to seek the help of a specialist consultant if the grounds for dismissal might appear a touch shaky!

9
TRAINING YOUR STAFF

Proper staff training is the key to your success.

It is essential, for the success and the safe running of your business, that your staff all know why and how a job has to be done. Good training helps them to give quality service, and to reduce the number of accidents in the workplace.

It is also necessary for your staff's well-being that you help them develop their potential and improve their skills. If they can do their jobs well they will have greater job satisfaction.

Training staff on the job

When you find someone you think is a suitable employee you should arrange to train them on the job. This can be done by yourself or, if you have a particularly competent employee, he or she can do it for you. In-house training ensures that your standards are instilled from the beginning and you can judge how well your new employee works.

Do consider the following when training your staff:

☐ Put the employee at ease so that they feel comfortable with you.

☐ Ask what they already know about the job.

☐ Give them an explanation, a demonstration, and practise with each task.

Sometimes, if you are training staff to take orders and wait on tables, role-playing is helpful. First the member of staff plays the part of the customer and you take their order. You then reverse the roles and you become the customer and ask the trainee to take the order.

☐ Before you move on to the next step, make sure that what you have shown the trainee has been understood – if not, show them again.

☐ Ask your employee to try to do the task themselves. Again, if they are having problems with it, repeat your demonstration slowly.

☐ Encourage them to ask questions if they are not sure about anything.

☐ Be prepared to answer questions accurately and, if you don't know all the answers, admit it and promise to find out. Try to anticipate the sort of questions you may be asked, so that you will have your answers ready.

☐ Never ask an employee to do something that you wouldn't do yourself.

☐ Treat each employee as an individual.

☐ It is a good idea to send members of staff to a local college for basic environmental health training. This will give them useful knowledge about hygiene and safe handling of food. They will also be awarded a certificate, which will instil in them a sense of pride and achievement.

USING AN OUTSIDE AGENCY

You don't have to offer in-house training as there are agencies that undertake training on a day-release basis. Contact your local authority or local college for information.

Compiling a staff manual

An idea is to write a staff manual which you can print out and then give a copy to each new member of staff before they start work. Make sure they do read it. If you have two members of staff starting at the same time, one way of reinforcing the contents of the manual is to ask them a few questions on it or have a quiz. This might be daunting for one member of staff alone, so instead you could ask them if they have any questions on the manual or if they need anything clarified.

An advantage of using a staff manual is that it ensures that all your staff have the same basic level of understanding. This is very important if you want to give high-quality service to your customers.

A copy of the staff handbook which I used in my coffee shop can be found in Appendix 5. My staff manual was fairly formal and included procedures and consequences in relation to:

☐ sexual harassment;

☐ bullying;

☐ drug and alcohol abuse;

☐ bad timekeeping;

☐ failure to show up for work;

☐ procedures for disciplining a member of staff;

☐ all regulations and guidelines employees should know.

You may wish to consider some of these when compiling your own manual or handbook.

Your manual should include the following:

Timekeeping: This is very important; if one member of staff comes in late on a regular basis it causes discontent with other employees. Staff should be ready to start work with their aprons on at 9 a.m. and not just arriving at 9 a.m.

Cleanliness and appearance: Everything you need to know about cleanliness is detailed in the Environmental Health Office manual. This is available from your local authority (see page 96). Include the form of dress required and the importance of tying back long hair.

Professional behaviour: Impress upon staff the importance of constant awareness of one's responsibilities when dealing with both the public and colleagues.

General care: After clearing dirty dishes from a table, the table should always be wiped with a spray cleaner and covered with a clean cloth ready for the next customer. If staff are clearing a table where a customer is still sitting, they should ask them first of all if they are finished and then if they would like the member of staff to get them anything else.

Staff should wipe down the chairs and make sure that they clean all rubbish from the floor.

They should examine sugar dispensers and salt and pepper pots to make sure they are not empty and the lids are securely screwed on.

Following up training

Remember that staff require ongoing training as they sometimes pick up bad habits and these should be corrected before they are passed on to new members of staff.

Review your staff performance every three or four months. This will help them to stay motivated and to continue to give your customers excellent service.

Teaching staff how to generate good customer relations

Your staff must learn the art of greeting a customer in a way that makes the customer feel valued and special. Staff should acknowledge their customer no matter how busy they are. As well as giving a verbal greeting, they should smile and make eye contact. A warm, genuine smile that reaches their eyes as well as their mouth will show the customer that he or she is important to the staff.

HOW YOUR STAFF CAN HELP YOUR BUSINESS

You want your staff to increase the amount of money the customer spends in your coffee shop by making a suggestion or a recommendation. For example, when taking an order for coffee, your staff could try to promote an item by asking the customer if he or she would like to try today's special sandwich or one of the newly baked scones which are just out of the oven and still hot. This is important to the success of your business and you will lose money if your staff don't take these opportunities.

The attitude of your staff plays an important part in building and maintaining your business. If they appear happy and enthusiastic and give great service the customer will be won over and will return to your coffee shop. Respect your staff and praise them when they work well and they will become one of your most effective forms of public relations.

Dealing with difficult customers

Sometimes, despite the best efforts of the staff, a customer may complain about something he or she is not happy with. You will have to be diplomatic in this type of situation and although you may often think that the problem is not your fault, you will on most occasions have to let the customer win. An unhappy customer will tell an average of 10 people about his or her experience. You want to ensure that your customers leave with a positive impression of your coffee shop.

TURNING THE SITUATION TO YOUR ADVANTAGE

Customers are looking for quality service and if you do not provide this you will risk losing them and may eventually lose your business. However, in some cases you can turn a complaint into something positive by listening to the complaint and learning from it. You will also feel a sense of satisfaction if you can solve your customer's complaint satisfactorily.

Some difficult customers you may encounter are:

☐ the angry customer who is upset and emotional about the incident;

☐ the demanding customer who is insisting that something be done immediately;

☐ the intimidating customer who is showing hostility by talking loudly, making sarcastic remarks and perhaps pointing a finger at a member of staff.

Different as they are, all these customers feel that they have been wronged and they are upset and emotional about it.

DEFUSING THE SITUATION

First of all ask your customer to move to a quiet place in the coffee shop and instruct your staff not to interrupt you. Then try to defuse the situation by:

☐ staying calm and not losing your temper;

☐ letting your customer talk;

☐ listening to what they have to say;

☐ gathering information;

☐ not taking the complaints personally.

Stay calm and listen

Listen carefully to what your customer has to say without interrupting and at the same time try to read their body language. Allow them to air their feelings and get rid of some of their anger. Don't say anything in return; instead just nod occasionally and make eye contact to show that you are listening and paying attention to them. Remember that your body language will also convey to the customer how you are feeling so don't stand with your hands on your hips in a confrontational manner. Watch the tone of your voice, too.

Put yourself in your customer's shoes

Put yourself in your customer's shoes and say that you understand how they feel about the incident, although you don't have to agree with them. Summarize in your own words what you understand the problem to be, and be sincere because you don't want your customer to feel as if you are patronizing them. This lets your customer know that you have been listening to what they have said. When the customer sees that you care about the problem they will probably begin to calm down.

Don't blame anyone for the incident or mistake.

RESOLVING THE PROBLEM

Learn as much as possible about the situation before you attempt to find a solution. When you have gathered all the information you need you can begin to resolve the problem. Your customer will appreciate your dealing with their complaint quickly and in a professional manner.

Thank the customer for bringing the incident to your attention and assure them that you will make sure that it doesn't happen again. At this stage you could offer your customer a refund and a complimentary coffee the next time they visit your coffee shop. Or you could ask them what you could do to compensate them for any inconvenience they have been caused. Personally, I would rather use the first solution because if you ask someone what you can do to compensate them they usually say that they are not looking for anything.

If you stay calm and reasonable, there is a good chance that you will placate your customer. If you offer a complimentary coffee, they may return.

DON'T TAKE IT PERSONALLY

Sometimes a complaint can be the fault of a member of your staff; however, it may just be that the customer is a constant complainer, or is in a bad mood about something else, or even simply trying to get a free coffee or meal. Don't take the complaint personally, act in a professional manner and remember that 'the customer is always right'.

It is a good idea to keep a note of customers' complaints. Include:

☐ the date and time of the complaint;

☐ the customer's name and address;

☐ the nature of the complaint.

This will enable you to see if the same complaint comes up more than once, and who was working on the dates concerned. You can then talk to staff and try to prevent the situation happening again. If you have the customer's name and address, send them a voucher for a free coffee when you are doing your next promotion.

'*We had a customer who ordered a baked potato with a chilli con carne filling (we always give a generous portion). She ate most of the filling and then sent the meal back to the kitchen, complaining that there was too little filling in the potato. It was easier just to give her an extra portion of the filling, even though I felt that she did not have a reason to complain.*'

If a customer is abusive don't react as they will use this to justify their behaviour and become even more abusive. Keep calm and ask them to tell you what the problem is. If they continue to use abusive language, tell them that you will have to ask them to leave.

'*I was in a restaurant recently and a customer started shouting loudly that he wasn't happy about his bill. The young girl who was serving him spoke quietly and when he continued being abusive she walked away and asked the manager to take over. He politely asked the customer to leave the restaurant and then left the table. The man sat for another five minutes before getting up and putting his coat on. Before leaving the restaurant, he turned and looked at the member of staff in a threatening manner. For a moment it looked as if he was going to go back and say something else but he decided against it and left. In my opinion the staff handled the situation well, remaining calm and polite.*'

Organizing regular staff meetings

Staff meetings are important to staff development and morale. They give everyone a chance to raise matters which concern them. It is better to get any problems out into the open and try to find a solution for them.

You will probably have to hold meetings after the shop has closed to allow all members of staff to attend and ensure there are no interruptions from customers.

☐ Set a date and time limit for the meeting;

☐ Before the meeting circulate a sheet of paper among your staff for them to write on it what they would like to discuss;

☐ Compile an agenda from the staff suggestions, including items you would like to discuss, and stick to it (this is a good opportunity to discuss such problems as bad timekeeping).

Tackling absenteeism

One of the worst problems I have encountered is absenteeism in the workplace. Staff, including weekend workers, telephone in the morning to inform you that they will not be coming to work because they are 'sick'. Sometimes they just don't turn up at all. (I often wonder how they always manage to be sick on working days after they have been out late the night before!)

Some absences will be a result of genuine sickness but recent research has found that the average sick leave for an employee is 8.7 days per year. There are certain professions that have a greater problem than others, and the catering business appears to be one of them.

I feel strongly about absenteeism by workers and I am convinced that since self-certification of sickness came into force absenteeism in the workplace has significantly increased. Workers can simply phone in 'sick' if they feel like a day or two off work.

It is reported that 20 million sick notes are written by GPs each year and as many as 5 million of these are believed to be bogus. This has given rise to the belief in the 'sick note' culture of Britain.

 **TIP** Do not pay anyone who is off work sick. If they are genuinely unwell they will be able to claim sickness benefit. Their contract of employment should state clearly that they are not entitled to payment when they are off work because of illness. To pay them could well send a confusing message to staff and may set an unfortunate precedent.

There are steps you can take to tackle absenteeism.

☐ Keep a record of sick leave, when and why a member of staff has been off work.

☐ Let your staff know that if someone keeps taking time off from work they are putting other members of staff under pressure, and if they repeatedly take time off without a genuine reason then you will have to take disciplinary procedures.

☐ Return to work interviews can be an effective way of tackling absenteeism. Interview your employee when they return to work to try to discover and address any problems they may have that have caused their absence.

☐ Look at your employee's contract of employment to see what action can be taken for repeated absence. You can request that your employee gives you a sick note obtained from their doctor, and if they are off for a considerable time you may be able to ask them to have a medical carried out by an independent doctor.

 It is a good idea to employ a floating member of staff who can be on standby to cover sickness at short notice as well as holidays. You can guarantee that there will always be someone off for sickness or holidays.

Hanging on to good staff

People working in a coffee shop don't tend to stay in the job for very long. Sometimes though, you will get someone who will continue to work for you for a number of years. I have found that the staff who stay longer and who are more committed are women returning to work after bringing up their children. They often prefer to work part-time.

 I often think that two good part-time workers are worth more than one full-time person who has no commitment to the job. Also part-time workers can often fill in for each other for holidays or sickness.

INSTILLING A SENSE OF LOYALTY

Once you have trained your employees, how do you keep your staff happy and productive and how do you instil a sense of loyalty in them?

☐ Offer competitive salaries;

☐ Pay a Christmas bonus;

☐ Allow them day-release to train and obtain a qualification;

☐ Provide a great-looking uniform;

☐ Initiate a worker of the month scheme where the winner gets a gift or bonus;

☐ Praise your staff for good work;

☐ Offer a chance for promotion within the business.

 **Don't get too familiar with staff as you might find it difficult to give criticism or discipline them. They do not have the same interest in the business as you have or any particular loyalty unless they have a share in it. Quite often they will move on to another job if the pay or hours are better.**

LEARNING TO BE A GOOD BOSS

Employees work better for a good boss – that's a fact. To get the best from your staff you must earn their respect by setting an example that they can aspire to. Always be polite, fair and behave towards them with integrity. Let them know that you care about their welfare and appreciate their efforts.

Communication

Be careful how you express yourself to your staff. Your feelings are conveyed by your body language, attitude, tone of voice and the words you use when talking to them. Try to be patient and remember when you are giving them instructions that not everyone can process information in the same way; some people have to be shown a task several times before they understand how to do it properly.

What you should do:

☐ **Do** be patient with your staff and try to use positive rather than negative words when talking to them.

☐ **Do** try to be good-humoured and create a happy working environment.

☐ **Do** make sure that you can plan, organize and delegate jobs that have to be done in the coffee shop.

☐ **Do** try to build a feeling of teamwork; your staff will work better in a contented team.

☐ **Do** think of yourself as part of the team and contribute significantly.

☐ **Do** make yourself available when one of your employees needs help and guidance.

☐ **Do** inspire confidence.

☐ **Do** listen to your employees and try to see issues from their point of view.

☐ **Do** treat seriously any ideas of you staff to improve your business.

☐ **Do** help your employees to develop their skills.

☐ **Do** recognize good work and achievements and give praise for tasks done well.

☐ **Do** always concentrate on improvements and not on shortfalls.

☐ **Do** thank all your staff at the end of the day for the good work they have done.

What you should not do:

☐ **Don't** try to do everything yourself because you may make your employees feel that they are not good enough to do the task themselves.

☐ **Don't** criticize a member of staff in front of other employees or your customers. If you have something to say to them, ask them to wait behind or take them into another room.

☐ **Don't** demean an employee as a form of punishment.

☐ **Don't** shout at your staff.

☐ **Don't** show favouritism.

Finally, I've said this before but it's worth repeating: never ask a member of your staff to do something you wouldn't do yourself.

10
COMPLYING WITH HEALTH, SAFETY AND HYGIENE LAWS

Now that you have opened your coffee shop and found good staff to help you run it, one of your top priorities is keeping your shop spotlessly clean at all times. This is not just to keep it looking good, it is essential for the health and safety of your customers and your staff, and the success of your business.

Be committed to cleanliness

You have a legal requirement to keep your shop clean and hygienic. Any shop that serves food and drink must maintain very strict standards of cleanliness and hygiene. If you do not, you will not only risk losing customers to your competitors, you could risk making them sick from food poisoning. Your business can be closed down by the Environmental Health Department of your local authority if you do not satisfy legal requirements.

Effective cleaning helps prevent bacteria from spreading from hands, equipment and surfaces. Train your staff to use quiet periods to keep on top of all essential cleaning tasks. They should always be aware of items that constantly need to be cleaned, and when the shop is quiet they can take the initiative on such jobs as wiping trays, cleaning finger-marks off the doors or wiping out the fridge.

It is a good idea to make out a cleaning schedule for equipment and surfaces that have to be cleaned each day and for areas which need to be attended to less frequently. Do have your schedule laminated and fix it to the wall of the kitchen. Make another list to be initialled by the member of staff who carries out each job. If the job has not been done satisfactorily you will know who carried it out. It would surprise you how many times I have heard 'I didn't do that job' or 'That isn't my job'. To avoid disputes you can make certain members of staff responsible for cleaning a specific area each night.

Always use antibacterial, food-safe chemicals; and use colour-coded cloths – a different colour for cleaning different areas or equipment.

Drawing up a cleaning schedule

Here is a sample cleaning schedule you could use. This routine should be carried out each night after you have closed the shop.

COFFEE SHOP AREA

☐ Wipe down seating areas, tables and chairs;

☐ Wipe trays and stack neatly;

☐ Wipe over serving counter;

☐ Empty rubbish bins, wipe out with disinfectant and replace old bin liner with a fresh one;

☐ Check cutlery is clean and has been polished with a clean cloth;

☐ Tidy magazines and remove old newspapers;

☐ Fill all sugar containers, salt and pepper pots, napkin and straw dispensers;

☐ Vacuum carpet or sweep and mop floor.

TOILETS

☐ Clean toilets with toilet brush, put bleach down the pan and leave overnight;

☐ Empty rubbish bins and wash with disinfectant;

☐ Clean sinks and fill soap dispensers;

☐ Restock toilet rolls;

☐ Brush and mop floor;

☐ Switch off lights and extractor fans.

 **Check that the lights have been turned off in the toilet area. Although I continually remind staff that they must be turned off after all the cleaning has been completed, there have been occasions when I have come to work to find the lights have been left on overnight.**

KITCHEN AREA

☐ Thoroughly clean dishwasher as per manufacturer's instructions;

☐ Empty rubbish bin, wash it out and place a fresh bin liner inside it;

☐ Clean microwave;

☐ Clean oven and hob;

☐ Clean sinks with appropriate cleaner;

☐ Sweep and mop floor;

☐ Wipe all surfaces and doors;

☐ Wipe down fridge and freezer doors.

FRONT OF SHOP AND COFFEE AREA

☐ Clean cake cabinet and wipe down counters;

☐ Backflush coffee machine as per manufacturer's instruction and clean all other parts, including the drain tray and the filters;

☐ To keep drainage of coffee refuge unobstructed, pour a jug of boiling water down the drain box;

☐ Scrub the milk steaming jugs with steel wool;

☐ Empty and wash filter coffee pot;

☐ Brush and mop floor.

Ask your staff to carry out other tasks like wiping out the fridge and the drinks chiller, cleaning windows and dusting window ledges when they are not busy serving customers.

If you have a washing machine on the premises, designate a member of staff to collect the dish towels and washing cloths at the end of the day and put them in the washing machine so that they are ready to be dried the following morning.

Tips for effective cleaning

☐ Do not use sponges in the kitchen as they provide one of the friendliest environments for bacteria, allowing them to multiply rapidly.

To help your staff to use a separate cloth for different areas to be cleaned, buy different-coloured cloths, e.g. blue for the toilets, yellow for tables and green for the fridge. Never use the same cloth you use for cleaning the microwave to clean the rubbish bin or the floor.

☐ Microfibre cloths come in five colours in packs of 10, containing two cloths of each colour. You can buy them from www.micro-pro.co.uk at about £5 for a pack of 10. These cloths can be used dry for dusting or wet for cleaning. They are hard-wearing, tough, very absorbent, easily kept clean and will last for a long time.

☐ Always use antibacterial food-safe chemicals for cleaning, and disinfect your cleaning cloths regularly.

☐ Milk steaming jugs have to be scrubbed with steel wool each night and then put through the dishwasher to get rid of the hardened milk which has built up during the day.

☐ Make sure staff keep all areas of your baking display case immaculately clean, especially those parts seen by customers when they are standing in front of them. Serving tongs and other utensils should be kept clean at all times. All bakery products should be removed from the display case before you clean it in order to protect them from any of the cleaning materials.

☐ If you use thermal jugs for keeping filter coffee warm you cannot submerge these in water. Clean them by letting them steep overnight using a solution of baking soda and hot water. For stubborn stains use a long-handled brush to scrub the inside and simply wipe clean the outside. You must always remember to rinse them out thoroughly before you use them again.

☐ Do show your staff which cleaning products to use and how they should be diluted and stored.

FLOORS

Ask your staff to sweep the floor throughout the day and to mop up any spills that may occur. Sweep and mop the floor last thing every night so that your customers and staff are not walking over wet floors. Wash with hot water and the appropriate cleaning solution (as approved by the Environmental Health Office). Wash out the mops and leave them to dry overnight.

KITCHEN AREA

The kitchen area should be spotless and this requires continual cleaning by staff. Washing down areas and equipment is common sense but sometimes you have to keep reminding staff to do this.

☐ Keep walls and extractor fans clean by washing them down regularly;

☐ Empty rubbish bins throughout the day as you don't want them to overflow;

☐ Keep the floor free of debris by sweeping regularly throughout the day;

☐ Make sure you have antibacterial soap available on each washbasin for staff use. It is essential that staff wash their hands before handling any food items, after emptying the rubbish bin, and especially after going to the toilet or handling money.

WASHING DISHES

A dishwasher is a more hygienic way of washing dishes than washing them in the sink. Follow the manufacturer's instructions and use the recommended cleaning and rinsing solution. First rinse off any food particles left on the dishes before loading them into the machine. Pans usually have to be scrubbed before putting them through the dishwasher as the machine won't remove stubborn stains or baked on food.

If you don't have a dishwasher you will have to use the double sink method. Rinse off the particles of food, wash the dishes in hot soapy water with a detergent approved by the Environmental Health Office, rinse them in clean hot water and then allow them to drip dry.

> *Believe me when I say that a dishwasher is a godsend.*

 Inform your staff that when they are handling mugs, cups and glasses they should not touch the rims with their hands. When handling cutlery they should only touch the handles.

TOILETS

□ Make sure the toilets are checked regularly throughout the day;

□ Keep toilet paper and paper hand towels (if used) well stocked;

□ Make sure bins are emptied when they are full;

□ Keep soap dispensers topped up.

Working with your local Environmental Health Department

When you are planning to start a coffee shop, you should contact the Environmental Health Department of your local authority. An officer will come to your premises and give you advice and information about what you will need to do before opening to comply with the legal requirements. They will also give you information on how to register your premises. Try to build up a good relationship with your local Environmental Health Officers; their advice can be invaluable, especially when you are planning a new business.

If you are considering taking over an already established coffee shop it may be worth your while contacting your local Environmental Health Department to invite them to look over your shop to see if it requires updating or anything renewing. The officer will give you advice and guidance about what you can and cannot do to the premises. This also gives you an idea how much money you will have to spend on the premises before you can open for business.

You can obtain information on preparing and serving food in booklet form from your local Environmental Health Department. You can also obtain up-to-date publications on food hygiene, 'A Guide for Businesses' and 'Starting Up' from the Food standards Agency at www.food.gov.uk or telephone 0845 606 0667. The Food Standards Agency is a UK-wide independent government agency which provides advice to the public and the government on food safety, diet and nutrition.

REGISTERING YOUR BUSINESS

Before opening your coffee shop, you are required by law to register your business with the Environmental Health Department of your local authority. You must register your business at least 28 days before opening. This applies to most types of food businesses, including catering run from home, or temporary premises such as stalls and vans.

If you use two or more premises you will need to register all of them. For example, if you are going to use the kitchen in your own home for baking or making up any fillings for sandwiches to sell in your coffee shop, you must also register these premises.

You must always inform your local authority if you make any significant changes to the way you run your business.

Complying with the rules and regulations

You are required by law to comply with the following rules and regulations.

PREMISES

☐ Your premises must be suitable for the purpose of your business;

☐ The premises must be suitable for preparing food safely;

☐ You must keep your premises clean, in good repair and well maintained at all times;

☐ You must be able to follow good hygiene practices including protection against contamination;

☐ To prevent contamination from the spread of disease, you must carry out integrated pest control.

HAND WASHING FACILITIES AND TOILETS

You must have enough hand wash basins for your staff to wash and dry their hands and they must have hot and cold running water. You must provide an approved antibacterial hand wash for staff to wash their hands, and materials for drying them hygienically.

Paper towels are more hygienic than fabric towels. You can purchase a unit and rolls of paper towels from a company selling janitorial items, or you can simply fit a domestic fitment and ordinary kitchen roll yourself.

□ There must be sufficient toilets, and these must not communicate directly with the area where food is being prepared.

□ You must also have adequate ventilation, lighting and drainage.

□ You must store disinfecting and all cleaning chemicals away from the food handling area.

FLOORS, WALLS AND DOORS

□ The floor in your kitchen must be well maintained and in good condition and should be easy to clean and disinfect.

□ The surface of the floor should be made of materials that do not allow fluid to pass through it, washable and non-toxic.

□ Walls and doors should be easy to clean and should be smooth and hard-wearing and in a good state of repair.

SURFACES

□ In areas where food is being handled, surfaces (including surfaces of equipment) must be easy to clean, in good condition and, where necessary, be able to be disinfected.

□ Surfaces should be smooth, washable, corrosion-resistant and non-toxic, e.g. stainless steel.

WASHING EQUIPMENT AND FOOD

□ Your shop must have adequate facilities and a good supply of hot and cold water for cleaning, disinfecting and storing utensils and equipment.

□ Your shop must have an adequate supply of hot and/or cold water available for every sink used for washing food.

FOOD WASTE AND RUBBISH

□ You must remove rubbish and food waste from your kitchen as quickly as possible.

□ Do not let bins overflow in the kitchen.

□ You must have adequate facilities for storing and disposing of rubbish and food waste because there are specific rules about how certain foods must be collected and disposed of. Contact your local authority for details of how this should be done.

☐ You must be able to keep the storage area clean and free from animals and pests.

WATER SUPPLY

☐ You must have an adequate supply of 'potable' (drinking quality) water available and it must be used when washing food to ensure that contamination does not occur.

If you are going to use ice in your coffee shop it must be made using potable water.

Inspections by the Environmental Health Officer

An Environmental Health Officer will usually come to check your premises before you open your coffee shop and thereafter may visit every six months, or once a year. The Environmental Health Officer can turn up at any time and they do not tell you when they are coming. If a customer informs them that they have been ill after eating food in your shop, someone from the department will also visit you at that time.

WHAT IS THE INSPECTOR LOOKING FOR?

When the Environmental Health Officer visits your premises they will ask you or, if you are not present, a member of your staff a number of questions and check some of the following facilities:

☐ They will run their hand along the insides of cupboards for dust.

☐ They will check your kitchen, seating area, toilet facilities and cupboards or storage space.

☐ They may check that all the fillings in the fridge are in containers and are labelled and dated.

☐ They will ask to see a record of your food temperatures for reheating and keeping food hot.

☐ They will check that all freezer and fridge temperature charts are kept up to date.

☐ They will ask if you use the correct chopping boards.

☐ They will check that the kitchen is kept clean and in good repair.

☐ They will check that you have pest control measures in use.

☐ They will check that there are adequate hand wash facilities for the number of staff you have and the size of your kitchen.

☐ They will check that you have adequate rubbish bin and waste disposal.

☐ They will check that all food is stored above floor level and where there is no risk of contamination.

WHAT HAPPENS IF THERE ARE PROBLEMS?

You will receive written information about any problems, along with advice and guidance on how to rectify them. You will be given a reasonable time to put things right.

If you fail to comply with regulations relating to hygiene or to the processing or treatment of food, the inspector can serve an improvement notice on you. The notice must state the grounds on which the notice is served (i.e. in what way you are failing to comply), the contraventions and the time allowed to meet the statutory requirements.

If you are convicted of an offence under the regulations and the court is satisfied that the business involves an imminent health risk to your customers, the inspector can issue an emergency prohibition order which forbids the use of your premises or equipment.

You will be able to appeal the decision of the Environmental Health Inspector if you disagree with it and, if you are in this position, you should enquire what the procedures are.

Preparing and storing food safely

Anyone serving food in their coffee shop has a legal, commercial and moral obligation to provide food that is safe; that will not cause illness or food poisoning. Therefore you must ensure that the food you serve is protected from the risk of contamination.

Hygiene is more than mere cleanliness; it encompasses all measures necessary to ensure the safety of food during preparation, processing, manufacture, storage, transportation and handling. It is extremely important to train new staff in food hygiene and ideally this should be done as soon as possible after they start working with you. It would do no harm either to give your other staff a refresher course at the same time.

PERSONAL HYGIENE

☐ Staff working in food handling areas must maintain a high standard of personal cleanliness. They should wear suitable clean clothing and, where appropriate, protective clothing.

☐ Staff should keep their hair tied back (if they have long hair).

☐ Staff should not wear nail varnish, watches or jewellery when preparing food.

☐ Staff should not touch their face or hair, sneeze, eat or chew gum when they are working with food.

Any member of staff known or suspected to be suffering from any of the following should not be allowed to enter a food handling area:

☐ if they have a food-borne disease which could contaminate food with pathogens;

☐ if they have any infected wounds, skin infections or sores;

☐ if they have diarrhoea and/or vomiting.

Staff who are suffering from any of the above should contact the business owner or manager immediately.

 **You must purchase blue adhesive plasters and dressings to use on any cuts you or your staff might get when working with food. It is also advisable to have a burn relief spray or gel in the kitchen in case of accidents.**

Staff with diarrhoea or vomiting should not return to work until they have been symptom-free for 48 hours. You will have seen from the news how quickly norovirus (the most common cause of gastroenteritis) spreads.

HAND WASHING

Even though you give your staff food hygiene training, you may from time to time have to remind them why it is so important to know the basic rules.

Do make sure that your staff wash their hands thoroughly. This is essential to prevent harmful bacteria being transmitted from people's hands to food, surfaces and equipment. They should be particularly careful in the following circumstances:

☐ after a break or going to the toilet;

☐ before preparing and handling food;

☐ after blowing their nose;

☐ after scratching their head or touching their hair;

☐ after emptying the rubbish bin;

☐ after touching raw food;

☐ after sweeping the floor or cleaning.

THE COST OF POOR HYGIENE

☐ Poor hygiene and cleanliness in your coffee shop can result in the closure of your business by the local authority and the loss of your reputation.

☐ If you are found to be selling unfit food you can be fined and will have to pay legal fees because of contraventions of hygiene legislation.

☐ You could be sued by customers suffering from food poisoning.

☐ Staff will lose their jobs if your premises are closed down.

Do complete a formal course in Food Hygiene even if it is just a basic course to begin with. It is so important to have this knowledge.

COURSES IN FOOD HYGIENE

Some Environmental Health Departments offer formal courses at a reduced price for catering businesses. If you employ a large staff they will run a basic course on your premises.

You can also approach your local college to enquire about Food Hygiene courses. If you cannot afford to take time off work there is a basic course being offered through distance learning which you can do at home.

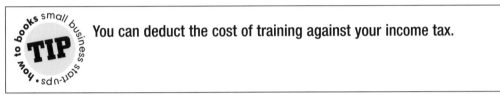 **You can deduct the cost of training against your income tax.**

All staff working in the food industry should be trained in the basic level of food hygiene within three months of starting work. The basic/elementary course is a one-day course lasting six hours with an exam at the end of it.

> *I had no informed knowledge about food and hygiene when I was planning to open a coffee shop so I signed up for a basic course in Food Hygiene and then an intermediate course which was going to take place two weeks later. Unfortunately, the first course was cancelled because there were not enough candidates and I had to go ahead with the intermediate course without any background knowledge. The course lasted a week and then there was a three-hour exam on the following Monday morning. It was really difficult for me because I had no food and hygiene background and most of the other people taking the course were either managers or owners of restaurants, work canteens and cafés. Fortunately I did pass first time. This gave me the Intermediate Food Hygiene Certificate of the Royal Environmental Health Institute of Scotland which is a second-level qualification in food hygiene, recognized nationally in all sectors of the food industry.*

If you follow the rules of hygiene and prevention of cross-contamination:

☐ there will be a reduced risk of food poisoning;

☐ your business will earn a good reputation for cleanliness and serving good safe food;

☐ you will be working within the rules and regulations of the food safety legislation.

Eradicating food hazards

In order to keep your coffee shop clean and the food you serve safe, it is necessary to put food safety management procedures in place. These procedures are crucial to ensure food safety. They are based on HACCP (Hazard Analysis Critical Control Point). A food hazard is any contamination which could cause harm to the consumer.

There are three classifications of food hazard: microbiological, chemical or physical.

☐ Microbiological could be, for example, bacteria present in or on food, or other micro-organisms that cause food poisoning;

☐ Chemical could be, for example, cleaning materials or insecticides;

☐ Physical could be, for example, glass or a hair clip.

Identify the areas where food hazards may occur. You will then need to put in place sufficient controls and to monitor procedures at those critical points in order to minimize risks. You must review your risk assessment and control procedures regularly and also whenever there is any change in the way you handle food. (Full details on identifying hazards and carrying out a risk assessment are on page 105.)

CHECKING AND ROTATING YOUR STOCK

Always check date marks on products when goods are delivered to you and return them immediately if:

☐ they are out of date;

☐ any of the packaging is damaged;

☐ frozen goods have started to defrost.

Make sure that you rotate your stock and check for out of date products on a daily basis. If any are out of date you must throw them away. This is a waste of food; however, if you rotate your stock properly you should not have this problem.

Never be tempted to serve out of date food to your customers.

> ❝ *I was in a coffee shop recently and picked up a packet of produce being sold in the shop and checked the date on it before going to pay for it. It was seven days out of date and there were a few other packets on the shelf also out of date. I brought this to the attention of the shop owner who didn't appear to be over concerned. This stock was obviously not checked on a regular basis. I am now wary of purchasing anything else from this particular coffee shop.* ❞

KEEPING FOOD AT THE RIGHT TEMPERATURE

One of my first tasks in the morning was to test the temperature of the fridges and freezers and record the reading on the appropriate chart. You are required to take a note of these temperatures twice a day.

Temperature controls are very important when you are storing food and also for cooking and reheating food. The Cook Safe Guide, developed by the Food Standards Agency Scotland, contains details of the different types of foods and the temperatures that apply to them. The Cook Safe system is also available in Chinese, Urdu and Punjabi. The equivalent used in England and Wales is 'Safer Food, Better Business' and in Northern Ireland it is called 'Safe Catering'.

These guides will give you all the information you require with regard to temperature control. You can get copies of each of them from your local authority and you can view 'Safer Food, Better Business' online at www.food.gov.uk/sfbb.

It is imperative that you keep foods at the correct temperatures so that you do not cause a risk to the health of your customers.

Cold foods

In England, Wales and Northern Ireland the legal requirement for food being kept cold is for it to be kept at 8°C or below. In Scotland the requirement is 5°C or below.

You will need to keep a temperature chart for inspection by the Environmental Health Officer. If you don't have a digital temperature display on the front of your fridge you should keep a fridge thermometer in the fridge at all times.

Keep a temperature chart on the door or side of your fridge to record daily temperatures of your fridge and freezers. If it is placed where staff can see it, it will remind them to check the temperature readings.

Hot food

There is a requirement throughout the UK that food being kept hot, for example soup, must be kept at 63°C or above.

There is a regulation in Scotland (apparently not in England and Wales) covering reheated food. Chilli con carne, for example, reheated in a microwave, has to reach 82°C. The exception is when such a temperature would be detrimental to the type of food; for instance, quiche could not tolerate this temperature.

Hot food which is not going to be served immediately should be cooled rapidly. However, it should not be placed immediately into the fridge as it could raise the fridge temperature and affect the food already stored there. Freshly cooked chilled foods have a maximum shelf life of five days and must be kept between 0°C and 3°C.

You will find that smaller portions of food put into shallow square containers will cool down more quickly.

Frozen food

Frozen food should be stored at −18°C

Put frozen food into the freezer as quickly as possible and do not allow it to remain at an ambient temperature for more than 15 minutes.

Do not overfill the freezer.

Do implement effective stock rotation and make sure that older food is used first to prevent waste.

If your freezer breaks down or food becomes thawed you may be able to treat it as fresh and in certain circumstances it may be cooked and refrozen. However, you should contact your local Environmental Health Department for advice on this.

LABELLING PRODUCTS CORRECTLY

If you buy in pre-packed sandwiches from a manufacturer to sell to your customers they must be labelled by the manufacturer with full details of ingredients and a 'use by' date. You will be in breach of regulations if the manufacturer has not labelled them correctly.

It is good practice to label the containers in which you store your fillings, stating what they are and on what date they were made.

Getting advice about health and safety issues

Every business, however small, has legal responsibilities to ensure the health and safety of employees and other people affected by the business, including customers, trades people, cleaners and suppliers.

First of all, as explained earlier in the chapter, you must register with your local authority. An Environmental Health Officer will visit your premises and advise you on what you need to do to comply with legal requirements. If you are just starting up in business and you want some help with health and safety in your workplace you can buy a Health and Safety Purchase Pack which provides a comprehensive, low-cost introduction to health and safety for new businesses.

The pack costs £30 and contains most of the basic health and safety advice you need. It also contains copies of the Health and Safety Law poster which must by law be displayed in your premises, and also the Health and Safety Executive Accident Book. For further information about Health and Safety the infoline telephone number is 08701 545500 and if you need to purchase any publications the website is www.hsebooks.co.uk or telephone 01787 881165. You can also download free leaflets from HSE's website www.hse.gov.uk

WHAT ELSE YOU SHOULD KNOW ABOUT HEALTH AND SAFETY

Insurance

You are legally required to have employers' liability insurance if you employ anyone. This is necessary to cover you in case someone takes legal action against you because they have been injured on your premises, owing to your negligence.

You must display a current certificate of insurance on your premises.

Ask your insurance broker to get you quotes for this type of insurance cover. The insurance company may want to visit your premises to make their own risk assessment.

First aid kit

You must keep a first aid kit on the premises and you must make sure all your staff know where it is kept.

Fire prevention equipment

You are required to have at least one fire extinguisher in good working order placed in the kitchen and, depending on the size of your premises, you might need to have another one in the sitting area of the coffee shop. You are also required to have fire blankets on the premises. You should contact your local fire prevention officer who will inspect your premises and advise you on what you require. You will have to get the fire extinguishers checked annually.

Carrying out a risk assessment

It is a legal requirement to carry out a thorough health and safety risk assessment to identify any potential areas of risk there may be in your coffee shop. This will minimize the risk of anyone having an accident on your premises or becoming unwell as a result of visiting your premises.

There are five main areas to look at when carrying out a risk assessment and these are:

IDENTIFY THE HAZARDS

☐ Check your premises to see if there are any significant hazards. You must check each section of your premises and take a note of anything you think may be a hazard.

WHO MIGHT BE HARMED?

☐ Consider everyone who works in your premises, your customers and people who will occasionally be on your premises, e.g. tradesmen or cleaners.

MINIMIZE THE RISKS

☐ Try to eradicate any hazards you have on your list or at the very least minimize or control the risk.

RECORD YOUR FINDINGS

☐ If you have five or more employees you will have to write down your findings and conclusions. If you have fewer than five employees you don't have to record them in writing. However, for your own information it might be helpful to make a list of significant hazards and what you need to do to get rid of the risk or minimize it.

PRIORITIZE YOUR ACTIONS

☐ You should prioritize the items on your list and carry out improvements on the most significant hazards first, especially those that could cause accidents or ill health. Once you have made all the improvements necessary, make sure that you keep a checklist to ensure that the control measures stay in place.

There are areas relevant to a coffee shop that you should check and I have listed a few below.

☐ Ensure that protective clothing such as aprons, and protective work wear such as oven gloves and rubber gloves, are provided.

☐ Check all electrical equipment is safe and, if it is not, get it repaired.

☐ Do not leave electric cables loose or trailing.

☐ Make sure that all floors are in good condition and that you put up a warning notice if they are wet and slippery.

☐ Ensure that all areas are well lit.

☐ Make sure that there are no objects left lying about where someone could trip over them. (This is one of the most common hazards in a coffee shop.)

☐ Provide adequate training to all your staff.

☐ Make sure that your staff have regular tea breaks.

☐ Ensure that all chemicals and cleaning substances are stored in the designated place.

☐ Look for any other areas where you think there may be hazards, and take steps to improve them.

REGULARLY REVIEW YOUR ASSESSMENT

Do review your assessment from time to time to make sure that your precautions are still effective and there are no new hazards that you need to deal with.

> *A member of staff in our coffee shop left the electric cable for the food mixer trailing on the floor and this was noted by the Health and Safety Inspector.*

It is your responsibility to train your staff to be aware of potential hazards and how to deal with them. Ask them if they know of any risks on the premises that have not been addressed; sometimes staff can be more aware of problems than you are.

Remember, it is not cost effective to ignore hazards that may be present on your premises. Complying with health and safety regulations will mean some expense for you, but it could cost you a lot more if a serious accident or illness occurs because of your negligence.

11
HOW TO INCREASE YOUR BUSINESS

Initially, when you are just starting your business, you will have to advertise quite frequently, and the amount you have to spend will seem quite high in relation to your turnover. Do work out how much you want to spend on marketing your business and stick to your budget.

I cannot emphasize strongly enough how important your staff can be in retaining customers and expanding your business. Train staff to welcome your customers with a smile and a 'Hello, nice to see you again'. People like to be recognized and if you make them feel valued they will return again and again.

Developing your marketing strategy

Your marketing strategy encompasses all your plans for increasing your sales. This entails attracting new people to visit your coffee shop and encouraging your customers to spend more per person and to return more often.

MEASURE RESULTS

You must measure the results of each strategy you use and if something doesn't work, don't try it again. Note in a diary the date and the type of promotion you have used. This will allow you to see if your turnover has increased after the promotion and by how much. If the promotion was successful then do it again at another time in the year. Particular occasions such as Valentines Day, Mother's Day, Easter or Hallowe'en are good times to choose for promotions.

AREAS YOU SHOULD CONCENTRATE ON

When you are developing your marketing strategy, you should concentrate on the areas detailed below:

□ Identify your market using the information you gathered when you were doing your original research (see Chapter 1).

□ Find out what your competition is doing to promote their coffee shop and create a strategy to improve on this and make your shop better and different.

□ Choose advertising methods that will be effective.

□ Research the costs of different types of advertising then set your advertising budget.

□ Make sure your advertisements reflect the character and image of your coffee shop effectively. Give thought to the way you word them; they must be enticing enough to tempt new customers to your shop.

☐ To assess the effectiveness of your advertising campaign you could use vouchers which must be handed in to your shop in exchange for a free tea or coffee. You will then be able to see if this particular type of advertising is working for you.

No matter where or in what way you advertise, your headline must be eye-catching and interesting enough to get the attention of your target market. A free gift or a discount is always an incentive to encourage new customers.

Using vouchers and flyers
VOUCHERS

One of the best ways to create new business is to offer a free coffee using vouchers. We have used this method of advertising several times and have found it to be quite effective.

Advertising in the local paper

If you advertise in your local paper people can cut out the voucher and exchange it for a free coffee. Alternatively you could offer a free coffee and 10% off other food ordered at the same time as the drink.

Working with a local business

Try approaching a local business, such as a gym, hairdressing salon, record store or anywhere else with a good customer base and ask them to hand out your vouchers to their customers. You could approach several businesses and use them at different times throughout the year. You may have to promote their business in return. This is a relatively inexpensive way of advertising, as you would only have to pay the cost of having the vouchers printed.

Counting the vouchers

You must remind your staff to collect the vouchers so that you know how successful your promotion has been and if it is worth repeating it. If you don't record the number of vouchers you have taken in during the promotion you won't know whether it has been successful or not, or whether it is the best way to attract new customers.

People love something for nothing and if the customer is getting a free cup of tea or coffee, more than likely they will purchase a sandwich or a cake to go with it. You are creating goodwill among local people and at the same time you are building up your customer base.

 If you are only offering a free coffee at a certain time during the day, do state this quite clearly on the voucher. Also state the 'valid from' and 'valid to' dates.

> ❛*Recently, like every other M&S cardholder, I received a voucher for a complimentary coffee with any purchase at any M&S café. I didn't notice on the voucher that the coffee had to be taken before 12 noon and I arrived at 2 p.m. and ordered a cappuccino and a toasted sandwich. The girl behind the counter pointed out that the voucher could only be used before 12 noon. The time was stated on the voucher but did not stand out and I admit that I had not read the details.*❜

I think M&S are quite clever when using marketing strategies, so let's look at the way they promoted their café:

☐ They offered a complimentary coffee or hot drink with *any purchase* in the café, so you had to buy something else from the café to get your free drink.

☐ They advertised on the voucher other items available in the café, for example, 'tempting pastries, fresh sandwiches, cakes and hot and cold drinks, it's the perfect place for breakfast, lunch or a quick snack. . . come and have a look!'

Your voucher should include:

☐ the name of your coffee shop, address and telephone number, and your logo (if you have one);

☐ **'FREE COFFEE'** in bold letters;

☐ details of the offer;

☐ some information on the other food and drink that you sell;

☐ coffee shop opening times;

☐ 'Valid from– to–' dates

If you are going to ask another business to give out vouchers for you, get quotes from a few printers before deciding which one to use. Then have the vouchers printed and deliver them personally to whichever business you are going to use.

If you are going to use the local newspaper for this type of advertising you may be able to come to an agreement whereby you will pay for an advertisement if they will do a story on your coffee shop free of charge.

FLYERS

You could design an attractive flyer that will appeal to the public.

Some of the things to consider include:

1. an attention grabbing headline;

2. making your offer sound irresistible;

3. eye-catching colours;

4. your layout;

5. your method of delivery.

☐ Head the flyer with the offer; this could include a free coffee, or coffee and a scone or cake at a discounted price during the quietest time in your shop. You could also offer a free mug or, at Christmas time, a free diary. Have your logo and the name of your shop printed on the gifts, to remind your customers of your coffee shop.

☐ List the tempting food and drinks you sell.

☐ Make sure the name of your coffee shop, address and telephone number are prominently displayed. Include your logo (if you have one).

☐ Give your coffee shop opening times.

☐ Have your flyer printed in eye-catching colours or colours that match the colour theme or logo of your coffee shop.

Note: You can send out flyers that only contains information about your coffee shop and the food and drink you sell, but if you offer something free you are guaranteed to get more results from the promotion.

Distributing your flyers

Flyers can be distributed in several ways. You can have them inserted into your local newspaper, delivered by hand by someone you employ or by the post office. The price for distributing flyers through the local paper or the post office will vary. Do enquire about prices before you decide to go ahead with flyers. You will have to give the post office a few weeks' notice as they have a waiting list for this service.

Some more ideas for attracting customers

☐ The best method of advertising by far is word of mouth, so offer an exceptional service with a smile, value for money and a comfortable, relaxing immaculately clean environment. Customers like to feel important; train your staff to smile when they greet customers, ask them if they enjoyed their coffee, and say that they look forward to seeing them again. A happy customer will not only return, they will sing the praises of your coffee shop to others and you will soon be busier than you ever expected.

☐ Consider special deals and multibuys, especially good for increasing business during quieter times of the day. For example, offer a cup of coffee or tea and a scone for 99p at a certain time, or a 'buy a cake and get a free coffee' deal.

❑ Create loyalty in your customers. Ask for their feedback on a small form and, if they leave their name and address, you can build up a simple database and either email them or mail them once a month with a preferential special offer. This builds up trust and loyalty in your customers and encourages them to come back. When they receive these offers, they often feel as if they know you personally.

❑ A customer loyalty card is a successful way of encouraging customers to return. Ask customers to have their card stamped each time they purchase a cup of coffee in your shop, and when they have collected six stamps they will get a free cup of coffee. Your customers will more than likely purchase a cake, scone or sandwich to go along with their free coffee, so it is unlikely that you will be losing any money during the promotion. Don't ask customers if they want a card; instead, just present them with one. The cards will remind customers of your coffee shop each time they open their purse or wallet.

Do take the loyalty card from the customer after it has been stamped six times and present them with a new one. You could ask your customers to put a contact name and telephone number on the card. You could then have a monthly prize draw. As a prize, you could give a mug or an item bearing your logo on it, or a cake and a coffee the next time the customer visits your shop.

❑ Send out preferential vouchers or discount cards to staff that work for other companies in your area.

❑ If you can handle it, offer a takeaway service for these companies, or allow them to phone in their order in advance. Staff often have short lunch breaks and no time to wait in a queue.

❑ Give vouchers to your staff, friends and family to give to people they know to help build up your customer base.

❑ If you are in a busy shopping area, you could prepare trays of sample coffees and mini cakes and go out into the area offering the samples to the public, as well as money-off vouchers to attract them into your coffee shop.

❑ You could try offering cut-price drinks, such as 10p for a regular coffee (not cappuccino or speciality coffees) or tea. This would probably just cover the cost of your coffee, tea and milk. You will probably find that most people will purchase something else anyway. Often this will work better than a 'free' promotion.

❑ Offering free refills on all regular coffees and tea usually works well.

> *We once had five customers at one table who ordered two pots of tea and five cups and then asked for a free refill. They certainly got value for their money!*

☐ If you want to promote speciality drinks to make more profit, try offering a 'special drink of the day' at a reduced price. You could also do the same with items of food.

Handing out customer questionnaires

Always encourage feedback from your customers, good or bad. Just as a happy customer can help build up your business by spreading good words, an unhappy one can do just the opposite. If you have a problem customer, try to sort out their grievance there and then and don't let it escalate. A customer feedback questionnaire can give you valuable insights into the way your business is viewed.

I have given you a sample of a customer questionnaire in Appendix 6, but of course you will know what specific questions you want answered by your customers. Make it multiple-choice questions and leave a space for your customers to tick the appropriate box, and then space for them to leave their comments and ideas.

This is a good opportunity to collect customers' names and addresses for future promotions. The ideal way to do this would be to run a competition with prizes, or to offer those who return the questionnaires a discount if they join your loyalty programme.

Ask your customers to leave their contact details on the questionnaires and to post the forms into a box that you have located in a prominent position in your café. You can determine how often you need to draw a winner – once a week or once a month – from the number of entries in the box. The prize might be a bottle of wine, for instance, or a meal for two.

ENCOURAGING CUSTOMERS TO RETURN

The real beauty of this would be that you could write to all the other entrants, thanking them for their comments, and telling them that you are sorry they did not win the main prize this month, but they have won a 'free coffee' on their next visit, or something along those lines. This would encourage these customers to visit your coffee shop again within a relatively short time. It is always a good idea to give a cut-off date on any such offer; for example, within the next 14 days. Twenty-one days is too long a time and 10 days is not long enough.

DEALING WITH NEGATIVE FEEDBACK

If you get a particularly bad customer comment, it would be worth contacting that customer, if you have their details, to discuss the problem and to assure them that it won't happen again. You could also offer the customer a refund or a free lunch to make up for their bad experience. There could be nothing worse for your new coffee shop than a disgruntled customer telling others about their bad experience.

Urge customers to let you know if there is a problem so that it can be rectified, and encourage satisfied customers to tell their friends about your shop. You will always get one or two awkward customers; it is just a fact of dealing with the public. However, but you can do your best to be prepared for them and know how to appease them should the situation arise. See Chapter 9 on how to handle difficult customers.

Allow regular customers to try mini free samples of new items you have put on your menu. You could give them a voucher for 10% off their next purchase to encourage them back. However, put a 14-day expiry date on the voucher so that they will return during that time.

I sometimes make small samples of shortbread to give out with a cup of coffee or tea. This allows customers to try the shortbread and at the same time feel that they are getting something free.

Using local radio and newspapers

Advertising in a local newspaper or on a local radio station is much more effective than on a national one because their target audience will more than likely be your potential customers. However, advertising in newspapers and on radio is very expensive so you need to think very carefully about it and only spend what you can afford to lose. Alternatively, try to think up a unique and creative way to get free media coverage for your coffee shop.

FINDING A UNIQUE ANGLE FOR YOUR COFFEE SHOP

Send a press release about your coffee shop to your local newspaper and radio station; this is a great way to get free publicity. However, you may have to think up an unusual, interesting, even unique angle to get people in your community interested: for example, you are using your great-grandmother's 100-year-old recipe for the most delicious caramel apple pie. Or perhaps you have lived all your life in the USA and have just moved to this area to open a speciality coffee shop in an old garage or somewhere unusual. You could coincide the opening of your coffee shop with your silver wedding anniversary, your 30th birthday or another special occasion.

If you can afford the expense, hiring a celebrity or well-known band to open your shop would get you newspaper coverage and you would also attract quite a lot of people to the shop.

The offer of a prize for a competition run by your local radio station or newspaper should get you a free write-up and perhaps a photograph of your coffee shop. All you should have to pay for is the prize. I previously mentioned in Chapter 4 that a competition to name your coffee shop is an excellent idea to get you free publicity in your local newspaper.

FUND-RAISING FOR A CHARITY

One way to get free radio advertising would be to organize a fund-raising morning or afternoon for a local charity and ask one of your well-known suppliers, e.g. Coca-Cola, Pepsi cola, or your supplier of coffee beans, to provide some small prize. You could give cans of Coke, Pepsi or packets of coffee to your first 50 customers or you could make a small charge for them which would go to the charity.

Whatever you do, make your story clear and interesting enough to attract the attention of potential customers.

 If you are advertising on the radio, be very specific and clear about the message you want to get across. State who your are, what you are offering and where you are, for example, 'Get down to Mandy's coffee shop for the best breakfast in town. For just £2.99 you get the full works and a bottomless mug of tea or coffee. Mandy's is at 25 High Street, Anytown.'

 If you do get free radio or newspaper coverage it is a good idea to write to the journalist or presenter, thanking them for the great story they ran about your coffee shop. You could also include some vouchers for a complimentary coffee or lunch for two people, for them to give to some of their friends.

Using your local tourist board

You could contact your local tourist board to enquire if you can be included in their brochure. This is usually placed in the bedrooms of hotels and B&B establishments. In my experience you have to get your own page designed and printed for inclusion in the guide and then you also have to pay a sum of money to the tourist board. Check out the price of doing this first of all because it may not be the best or the most cost-effective way for you to advertise.

Using an outside agency

Should you or your team run out of ideas but would still like to break out and create something new you can always contact a facilitator to help you consider new ideas for expansion. In the past I have used Paul Wigley who can be contacted on 0777 805 8026 or paul@howmightwe.co.uk or www.howmightwe.co.uk. I have found Paul very helpful and he is prepared to chat on the telephone.

12
POPULAR COFFEE SHOP RECIPES

Soups

- ☐ Minestroni Soup
- ☐ Leek and Potato Soup
- ☐ Chicken and Rice Soup
- ☐ Split Pea Soup
- ☐ Lentil Soup
- ☐ Quick French Onion Soup
- ☐ Scotch Broth
- ☐ Cream of Cauliflower and Stilton Soup
- ☐ Cream of Celery Soup
- ☐ Parsnip and Chilli Soup
- ☐ Cream of Carrot and Coriander Soup
- ☐ Cream of Carrot and Ham Soup
- ☐ Cream of Mushroom Soup
- ☐ Cullen Skink
- ☐ Cream of Tomato and Basil Soup
- ☐ Croutons

Savoury recipes

- ☐ Breakfast Casserole
- ☐ Meat Loaf
- ☐ Quiche
- ☐ Leek and Smoked Haddock Quiche

Fillings or toppings for baked potatoes

- ☐ Chilli Con Carne
- ☐ Chicken Tikka
- ☐ Chicken Curry
- ☐ Coronation Chicken

Popular cake recipes

- ☐ Sweet shortcrust pastry
- ☐ Coconut Slice
- ☐ Oven Scones
- ☐ Carrot Cake
- ☐ Cream cheese icing
- ☐ Fruit Loaf
- ☐ Cranberry Nut Loaf
- ☐ Apple Spice Loaf
- ☐ Apple Spice Chocolate Chip Cake
- ☐ Sticky Toffee Buns
- ☐ Caramel butter icing
- ☐ Toffee sauce
- ☐ Cupcakes
- ☐ Butter icing
- ☐ Gingerbread
- ☐ Plain Sponge
- ☐ Quick and Easy Shortbread
- ☐ Fine Shortbread
- ☐ Empire Biscuits

Tray bakes

- ☐ Fudge Slices

- ☐ Rich Chocolate Shortcake

- ☐ Mars Bar Squares

- ☐ Millionaire Shortbread

- ☐ Strawberry Tarts

- ☐ Toffee Tarts

- ☐ Crispy Surprise

- ☐ Banoffee Pie

- ☐ Strawberry and Vanilla Cheesecake

- ☐ Scottish Tablet

- ☐ Vanilla Fudge

Home baking is something that really brings in customers as there are very few shops nowadays that bake their own cakes and tray bakes. Most coffee shops and tea rooms take the easy option and buy in. This tends to give them an appearance of sameness. If you can manage it, do bake for your coffee shop yourself. If this isn't possible, you should employ a good home baker to do it for you. There is no comparison between the taste of home baking and cakes bought in from a local bakery.

I have included a few recipes which I find popular. It would probably surprise you to discover that customers generally buy more of what I call plain baking, e.g. plain sponge topped with icing and filled with jam and cream, scones, shortbread, fruit loaf and empire biscuits rather than chocolate cake and cheesecake.

The recipe for tablet has been around for many years. My grandmother made it to sell in her shop and then my mother made it for the family. You can sell it either in slices or cut into small squares and give it to your customers to eat with their coffee. I never have any left at the end of the day!

Soups

The soup in our coffee shop is made fresh every day but I do know a coffee shop owner who makes soup in a large batch and freezes half of it to use at a later date.

I was always told that the secret of making tasty soup was to sauté the vegetables in a little butter to begin with. This appears to bring out their flavour.

CREAM SOUPS

I prefer to make cream soup with double cream but if you want to make a cheaper version you can use half the amount of stock and the other half milk, e.g. 600 ml (1pint) stock and 600ml (1pint) full cream milk and then thicken the soup with cornflour.

Knorr makes a range of Bouillon which comes in various flavours including vegetable, chicken, ham, lamb and beef. It is similar to stock cubes but comes in a large tub.

VEGETARIAN SOUPS

If you want to make the soup suitable for vegetarians, substitute the chicken or ham stock with vegetable stock.

When we first opened we made stock from either cooked chickens or hams but soon found out that it was time-consuming and we now use Knorr Bouillon for making stock for all our soups.

The following soups are easy to make and popular with our customers. I usually make a large pot of a run of the mill soup and a small pot of a cream soup every day.

Don't make too large a quantity of soup to begin with until you see how much you are likely to sell in a day. It is better to run out of something rather than to have to throw it away.

You should give your customers a soup portion of 250 ml to 300 ml each. The recipes below should give you approximately 12 – 14 portions of run of the mill soup and approximately 8 portions of cream soup.

Double the quantities of ingredients if you want to increase the quantity of soup you make, and if it is too thick add some more stock. If you don't know how much soup you will sell initially, you could make two large pots of run of the mill soup and if you do not use the second pot, you could freeze it or refrigerate it to use another day.

MINESTRONI SOUP

This is a very chunky soup but it tastes delicious.

400 g (14 oz) barlotti beans
4 large leeks, sliced and washed
6 carrots
250 g (9 oz) turnip
4 large potatoes
4 sticks celery
50 g (2 oz) butter, melted
250 g (9oz) uncooked ham, chopped, or bacon (optional)
3.4 litres (6 pints) ham stock (made from Knorr ham bouillon,
or vegetable bouillon if you want to make it suitable for vegetarians)
3 cloves garlic
6 tomatoes or a 400 g tin of chopped tomatoes
2 tsp mixed or Italian herbs
1 tsp sugar
2 oz butter
Salt and pepper to taste
Pasta, approx 125 g (4 oz) (spaghetti pasta is best), broken into 2 inch pieces
Parmesan cheese (optional)

1 Dice vegetables and sauté them in the melted butter for about 10 minutes or until soft.

2 Add the chopped ham and cook for a further few minutes.

3 Add ham stock, garlic, tomatoes and bring to the boil and then simmer for about 20 minutes.

4 Add the mixed herbs and sugar, then season to taste.

5 Add the pasta and bring back to the boil, stirring all the time.

6 Lower the heat and simmer for 5 minutes or until the pasta is cooked.

Optional Serve with some Parmesan cheese sprinkled on top of the soup, and a portion of garlic bread.

Variations Use tagliatelle or small pasta shapes instead of spaghetti, or haricot or butter beans instead of barlotti beans. I often use French beans as they are quite cheap and give the soup some more colour, and don't really alter the flavour.

LEEK AND POTATO SOUP

8 large leeks, washed and sliced
50 g (2 oz) butter
3.4 litres (6 pints) chicken stock
6 medium potatoes, chopped into large chunks
6 medium carrots, grated
2 bay leaves
Salt and pepper to taste
2 handfuls of parsley, chopped

1 Slice and sauté the leeks in butter for 10 minutes or until soft.

2 Add stock, potatoes, grated carrot and bay leaves.

3 Bring to the boil then turn down the heat and simmer for about 20 to 25 minutes.

4 Season to taste and remove bay leaves.

5 Add chopped parsley.

CHICKEN AND RICE SOUP

6 large leeks, washed and sliced
2 sticks celery, finely chopped
50 g (2 oz) butter
4.6 litres (8 pints) chicken stock
4 large carrots, grated
4 chicken breasts (or you can substitute chicken legs), finely diced
250 g (9 oz) American long grain rice
Salt and pepper to taste
2 handfuls parsley, chopped

1 Sauté leeks and celery in butter for 10 minutes or until soft.

2 Add stock, carrots and chicken.

3 Bring to the boil, then turn down the heat and simmer for about 15 minutes.

4 Add rice and simmer for another 10 – 15 minutes until the rice is cooked.

5 Season to taste.

6 Add the chopped parsley.

SPLIT PEA SOUP

1kg (2 lb) split peas
8 leeks
2 sticks of celery
500 g (1 lb 2 oz) potatoes, diced
50 g (2 oz) butter
1 ham bone
4.6 litres (8 pints) water or ham stock
2 handfuls parsley, chopped
Salt and pepper to taste

1 Steep the peas overnight in cold water, then drain.

2 Sauté leeks, celery and potatoes in butter.

3 Place ham bone in the pot with the vegetables and peas.

4 Cover with the water and bring to the boil.

5 Turn down heat and simmer until peas are cooked, approximately 1 hour.

6 Remove the ham bone, cool the mixture slightly and liquidize.

7 Strip the cooked ham off the bone and return it to the soup.

8 Add the parsley.

9 Season to taste and if you have used a ham bone you may also have to add some ham bouillon to increase the flavour of the soup.

Variations If you do not have a ham bone you can use ham stock instead and then add some cooked bacon or ham after liquidizing the soup.
For vegetarian soup, omit the ham and ham stock and use vegetable stock.

LENTIL SOUP

1kg (2 lb) leeks, sliced and washed
4 carrots
50 g (2oz) butter
6.9 litres (12 pints) ham stock
675 g (1 lb 8 oz) red lentils, washed
Salt and pepper

1 Slice the leeks, grate the carrots and sauté in butter for about 10 minutes or until soft.

2 Add ham stock and bring to the boil.

3 Add the lentils to the pot, bring gently back to the boil and then simmer gently for about ¾ – 1 hour, stirring occasionally to prevent the lentils from sticking to the bottom of the pan.

4 Season to taste.

5 If the soup is too thick just add some more stock or water.

Variations You can add chopped ham if you like but it makes the soup more expensive to make.

For a change you can add 2 large cans of Heinz tomato soup or some tomato purée to make the lentil soup into Tomato Lentil Soup.

For Garlicky Lentil Soup add 4 large garlic cloves when you add the stock, or add some chopped garlic sausage. You might find, however, that most of your customers don't like garlic and in that case you could make a small amount of it as 'soup of the day'.

QUICK FRENCH ONION SOUP

1kg (2 lbs) onions, sliced
25 g (1 oz) butter
2 tbs vegetable oil
50 g (2 oz) plain flour
4.6 litres (8 pints) chicken or beef stock
2 bay leaves
Salt and pepper to taste

---

❶ Sauté onions in butter and oil until soft.

❷ Stir in flour and cook for 1 minute.

❸ Stir in stock gradually and add bay leaves.

❹ Bring to the boil and then simmer for approximately 15 minutes.

❺ Season to taste.

Serve with croutons or garlic bread.

Variation You can sprinkle some grated Gruyère cheese over the soup and put it under the grill to melt. (This makes the soup a bit more expensive but you can charge more for it.)

SCOTCH BROTH

This is quite a filling soup.

---

4 large carrots, grated
1 large turnip, grated
2 large onions
3 large leeks sliced and washed
100 g (4 oz) butter
4.6 litres (8 pints) of lamb stock
500 g (1 lb 2 oz) broth mix (steeped overnight in cold water)
2 handfuls parsley, chopped
Salt and pepper to taste

---

1 Sauté carrots, turnip, onions and leeks in the melted butter.

2 Add the lamb stock and broth mix and bring to the boil.

3 Simmer for about 1 hour, stirring occasionally so that the soup does not stick to the bottom of the pan.

4 Add the parsley and simmer for another few minutes.

5 Season to taste.

6 If the soup is too thick, thin it by adding more stock.

7 Serve with crusty bread, or a bread roll and butter.

CREAM OF CAULIFLOWER AND STILTON SOUP

If you want to make a less expensive variation of this soup, add milk and use less cream.

---

1 kg (2 lb) cauliflower, chopped
4 sticks of celery, chopped
2 large onions, sliced
75 g (3 oz) butter
1.2 litres (2 pints) chicken stock
150 g(5 oz) Stilton cheese, chopped
Pinch of nutmeg
240 ml (8 fl oz) double cream or 600 ml (1 pint) milk plus 50 ml (2 fl oz) double cream
Salt and pepper to taste
Parsley to garnish

---

❶ Sauté cauliflower, celery and onions in butter.

❷ Add chicken stock and milk (if using) and simmer until the vegetables are almost cooked.

❸ Add Stilton cheese and cook for another 5 minutes.

❹ Cool slightly and liquidize.

❺ Put back into pan and add nutmeg and double cream.

❻ Heat slowly and season to taste.

To serve, sprinkle each serving with a teaspoon of parsley.

Variation You can substitute broccoli for the cauliflower and celery to make Broccoli and Stilton Soup.

CREAM OF CELERY SOUP

2 heads of celery, finely sliced
1 large onion, sliced
2 leeks, sliced and washed
100 g (4 oz) butter
1.2 litres (2 pints) chicken stock
240 ml (8 fl oz) double cream
Salt and pepper to taste

1 Sauté the celery, onion and leeks in the melted butter for about 10 minutes.

2 Add chicken stock and bring to the boil, then turn down to simmer for about 20 minutes. Cool slightly and liquidize, then return to the pan and heat gently.

3 Add cream and season to taste.

PARSNIP AND CHILLI SOUP

4 onions, sliced
8 parsnips, peeled, quartered and wood centres removed
100 g (4 oz) butter
2 large cloves of garlic, chopped
1.2 litres (2 pints) of chicken stock
½ tsp hot chilli powder (add more to taste if you like)
Salt and pepper to taste
240 ml (8 fl oz) double cream

1 Sauté onions and parsnips in the melted butter for about 8 –10 mins until they begin to soften, then add the chopped garlic and cook for another 2 minutes.

2 Add the chicken stock and chilli powder and cook until the parsnips are tender.

3 Cool slightly and then liquidize.

4 Season to taste and add more chilli powder if required.

5 Return to the pan and mix in the cream and heat through.

Serve with a swirl of cream on top.

Variation For a different flavour, instead of using chilli powder you can use curry powder.

CREAM OF CARROT AND CORIANDER SOUP

---

6 leeks, sliced and washed
1kg (2 lb) carrots, sliced or grated
100 g (4 oz) butter
2.3 litres (4 pints) chicken stock
A handful of fresh coriander, chopped (you can use ground coriander
but I think fresh tastes better), plus a little coriander or parsley to garnish
240 ml (8fl oz) double cream
Salt and pepper to taste

---

1 Sauté the leeks and carrots in melted butter for about 10 minutes until they soften.

2 Add chicken stock and bring to the boil.

3 Add chopped coriander and bring back to the boil, cover and simmer for about 20 minutes until the leeks and carrots are cooked.

4 Cool slightly and liquidize.

5 Return to the pan and add the cream, reheat gently and then season to taste.

Serve with a swirl of cream and a little chopped coriander or chopped parsley.

Variation You can omit the coriander and add fresh minced ginger root and a pinch of nutmeg to make Carrot and Ginger Soup.

CREAM OF CARROT AND HAM SOUP

4 onions, finely sliced
225 g (8 oz) bacon or ham, chopped
100g (4 oz) butter
2.3 litres (4 pints) ham stock
900 g (2 lb) carrots, sliced
240 ml (8 fl oz) double cream
Salt and pepper to taste
A little chopped parsley, to garnish

1 Sauté onions and chopped bacon together in butter until soft.

2 Add ham stock and carrots and bring to the boil.

3 Simmer and cook for about 20 minutes. Cool slightly and liquidize.

4 Return to the pan, add the cream and heat gently.

5 Season to taste.

Serve with a swirl of cream and a little chopped parsley.

CREAM OF MUSHROOM SOUP

2 onions, finely sliced
550 g (1lb 4 oz) mushrooms, finely sliced
100 g (4 oz) butter
1.2 litres (2 pints) chicken stock
240 ml (8 fl oz) double cream
Salt and pepper to taste

1 Sauté the onions and the mushrooms in butter for approximately 2 minutes, then cover and sauté for about 8 minutes.

2 Add stock and bring to the boil, then simmer for about 15 minutes.

3 Cool slightly and liquidize. Return to the pan and add the cream and heat gently.

4 Season to taste.

CULLEN SKINK

This is a Scottish smoked fish soup which is delicious.

---

2 onions, finely chopped
2 leeks, sliced and washed
50 g (2oz) butter
500 g undyed smoked haddock (fresh or frozen but, if frozen, defrost first)
2.3 litres (4 pints) full cream milk
2 bay leaves
4 large potatoes, chopped
150 ml (½ pint) double cream
Salt and pepper to taste
2 handfuls of fresh parsley, chopped

---

1 Sauté the onions and leeks in melted butter until soft.

2 Place the smoked haddock on top and add enough milk to cover the fish.

3 Add the bay leaves and simmer for 5 minutes.

4 The fish should now be cooked so lift it from the pan and set aside.

5 Add the chopped potato and remaining milk to the pan and simmer for another 20 minutes. While this is simmering remove any skin and bones from the fish.

6 Break the fish into flakes.

7 Remove the bay leaves and liquidize the milk and vegetable mixture.

8 Return mixture to the pan, add the cream and heat through gently.

9 Finally, add the flaked fish and season to taste.

Serve sprinkled with chopped parsley.

CREAM OF TOMATO AND BASIL SOUP

4 onions, sliced
100 g (4 oz) butter
4 x 400 g tins of tomatoes plus a little tomato purée
3.4 litres (6 pints) chicken stock
1 tsp sugar
A handful of fresh basil, chopped
240 ml (8 fl oz) double cream
Salt and pepper to taste

1 Sauté onions in melted butter until soft and then add tins of tomatoes and chicken stock.

2 Bring to the boil then simmer for about 15 minutes.

3 Add sugar and chopped basil and simmer for another 5 minutes.

4 Cool slightly and liquidize.

5 Return to the pan, add double cream and heat gently.

6 Season to taste and if you think the soup requires more tomato, add some tomato purée and check the taste again until you have added sufficient.

Serve garnished with chopped basil leaves.

CROUTONS

*Croutons add a finishing touch, served with some of the soup recipes.
It is best to bake them in the oven.*

Small cubes of white or brown bread
Olive or vegetable oil

1 Line a baking tray with baking paper.

2 Spread oil all over the baking sheet.

3 Arrange cubes of bread on the sheet and cover them with the oil by turning them over until they are evenly coated.

4 Bake in a preheated oven at 180°C (350°F), Gas Mark 4 for about 10 minutes.

Variation If you want garlic-flavoured croutons, mix some garlic powder with the oil before spreading it on the baking sheet.

Savoury Recipes

I have included some popular recipes that are easy to make and are highly profitable.

BREAKFAST CASSEROLE
Serves 6 – 8

---

4 slices of bread
450 g (1 lb) sliced sausage, or spicy sausage for a change
2 cups (225 g or 8 oz) strong Cheddar cheese, grated
6 large eggs
2 cups (600 ml or 1 pint) milk
1 tsp salt
Dash of pepper
1 tsp dry mustard

---

1 Tear up bread and place in a greased baking dish, 32.5 x 7.5 x 5 cm (13 x 9 x 2 in).

2 Brown and drain sausage meat. Spoon sausage over bread.

3 Sprinkle with grated cheese.

4 Beat together eggs, milk, salt, pepper and dry mustard.

5 Pour over the mixture in the baking dish.

6 Cover and refrigerate for 30 minutes. (It tastes even better if refrigerated overnight.)

7 Bake at 180°C (350°F), Gas Mark 4 for 35 – 40 minutes. The cheese will rise to the top during baking.

MEAT LOAF

1 kg (2 lb) minced beef
2 large onions
6 rashers of bacon, chopped
250 g (9 oz) mushrooms, chopped
Vegetable or olive oil
4 cups (450 g or 1 lb) fresh breadcrumbs (more if required)
2 handfuls fresh parsley, chopped
2 eggs, beaten
Salt and pepper to taste

1 Brown the mince and set aside.

2 Fry the onions and mushrooms in a little oil until soft.

3 Add the onions, mushrooms and breadcrumbs to the browned mince.

4 Add chopped parsley and bind with the eggs. Mix well.

5 Grease and line 2 x 1 kg (2 lb) loaf tins and fill with mixture. Cover the top with greaseproof paper to stop the top of the loaf forming a crust.

6 Cook in a preheated oven at 180°C (360°F), Gas Mark 4 for 45 mins to1 hour.

Serve sliced, hot with gravy, or cold with salad and crusty bread. (You will be able to get a good profit from this.)

QUICHE
For the pastry

---

250 g (9 oz) plain flour
142 g (5 oz) hard Stork margarine or butter
1 egg
20 ml (1 fl oz) cold water

For the filling
You can use various fillings but I find that this is the most popular one.
1 onion, chopped
4 slices of bacon, sliced
2 tomatoes
125 g (4 oz) medium Cheddar cheese, grated
1 cup (225 ml or 8 fl oz) double cream
½ cup (110 ml or 4 fl oz) milk
5 eggs
Salt to taste

To make the pastry

1 Sift flour into a mixing bowl.

2 Rub in margarine or butter, or mix in a food processor, until the mixture resembles fine breadcrumbs.

3 Whisk egg and water together and add gradually to the flour mixture until it comes together in a ball.

4 Cover with clingfilm and leave in the fridge for 30 min.

5 Roll out the pastry on a lightly floured surface.

6 Grease a 25 cm (10 in) flan dish and line with the pastry.

7 Prick the base and then bake blind at 200°C (400°F), Gas Mark 6 for approximately 20 minutes or until the pastry is a pale golden colour.

To make the filling

1 Sauté the onion until soft, and add the bacon strips and cook for a further few minutes until cooked.

2 Place onion and bacon on top of the pastry case.

3 Slice the tomatoes and lay them on top of the onion and bacon.

4 Sprinkle the grated cheese over the top.

5 Whisk the cream, milk and eggs together, add salt to taste.

6 Pour the mixture on top of the quiche.

7 Bake in a preheated oven at 180°C (350°F), Gas Mark 4 for 30 – 40 minutes or until the egg mixture has set and is a light golden colour.

Serve hot or cold with salad.

 **TIP** Place the flan dish containing the filling on a baking tray before you pour over the egg mixture. This will save you spilling any if it runs over.

LEEK AND SMOKED HADDOCK QUICHE
Make the pastry base as on page 134 in a 25 cm (10 in) flan dish

For the filling

450 g (1 lb) smoked haddock
300 ml (½ pint) milk
300 ml (½ pint) double cream
1 bay leaf
Pinch of nutmeg
6 black peppercorns
450 g (1 lb) leeks
50 g (2 oz) butter
4 eggs
25 g (1 oz) medium Cheddar or Gruyère cheese, grated

1 Poach the haddock in the milk and half the cream with the bay leaf, nutmeg and peppercorns for 5 mins.

2 Remove the fish, strain the poaching liquid into a jug and set aside to cool.

3 Remove any skin or bones from the fish and flake it.

4 Sauté the leeks in the butter until soft.

5 Place the leeks and the flaked fish on the pastry case.

6 Sprinkle the grated cheese on top.

7 Whisk together the eggs, poaching milk and remaining double cream.

8 Pour egg mixture on top of quiche.

9 Bake in a preheated oven at 180°C (350°F), Gas Mark 4 for 35 – 40 minutes or until the egg mixture has set and is a light golden colour.

Fillings or Toppings for Baked Potatoes

Baked potatoes are very popular because they are easy to prepare and fill. There are many varieties of toppings and I have listed below a few of the most popular, as well as some more unusual ones.

 Do use your imagination to create appetizing toppings and gradually add some of them to your menu. If they don't sell well, take them off the menu and introduce different ones.

VEGETARIAN OPTIONS

- ☐ Broccoli in a cheese sauce
- ☐ Broccoli, onions and sour cream
- ☐ Sour cream and chives
- ☐ Baked beans with grated cheese
- ☐ Cheese and leek
- ☐ Creamed garlic mushrooms
- ☐ Mature Cheddar cheese
- ☐ Coleslaw

NON-VEGETARIAN OPTIONS

- ☐ Chilli con carne, grated cheese and sour cream
- ☐ Bacon bits and sour cream
- ☐ Chicken mayonnaise or chicken, sweetcorn and mayonnaise
- ☐ Coronation Chicken
- ☐ Prawns with pineapple, mayonnaise and a sprinkling of paprika
- ☐ Chicken curry
- ☐ Steak strips with onions
- ☐ Smoked salmon and cream cheese
- ☐ Tuna, sweetcorn and mayonnaise
- ☐ Smoked haddock in a cream sauce

☐ Haggis

☐ Diced ham, onion, red peppers and mayonnaise

☐ Diced ham with sour cream and chives

CHILLI CON CARNE

2 kg (4 lb) beef mince
8 large onions, finely chopped
6 cloves of garlic, finely chopped
4 Oxo cubes
1 – 1¼ litres (2 – 2½ pints) water
300 g (11 oz) tomato purée
1–2 tsp hot chilli powder (start off with 1 tsp and then add more if required)
2 tsp sugar
2 x 400 g cans red kidney beans
Salt to taste

1 Brown the mince in a large pot.

2 Add finely chopped onion and garlic and cook for 5 minutes.

3 Crush Oxo cubes and add to 600 ml (1 pint) of boiling water, then add tomato purée.

4 Add all the liquid to the mince.

5 Add chilli powder and sugar.

6 Bring to the boil then turn down heat and simmer for about 1 hour (alternatively, you can cook it in a casserole in the oven).

7 Check how hot the chilli tastes and add more chilli powder if required.

8 Check to see if the mixture requires more water or more tomato purée.

9 Add the drained kidney beans and simmer for another 10 minutes.

10 Season to taste.

CHICKEN TIKKA

3 large onions, finely chopped
100 g (4 oz) butter
8 cloves garlic
2 tsp cumin seeds
2 tsp coriander seeds
8 cardamom pods
4 tsp turmeric
4 tsp ginger powder
2 tsp chilli powder
8 chicken breasts, chopped into cubes
600 ml (1 pint) chicken stock made from chicken bouillon
300 ml (½ pint) double cream
Salt to taste

1 Sauté onions in butter until soft.

2 Add garlic and spices and cook for a few minutes.

3 Add chicken and cook for about 5 minutes.

4 Add chicken stock.

5 Cover and simmer for about 20 minutes until chicken is cooked.

6 Remove from heat and add double cream.

7 Season to taste.

CHICKEN CURRY

4 onions, chopped
100 g (4 oz) butter
6 cloves of garlic, crushed (you can substitute garlic powder or lazy garlic)
2 tsp coriander
2 tsp ginger
1 tsp turmeric
8 chicken breasts, chopped into cubes
2 x 400 g tins chopped tomatoes
Pinch of sugar
25 g (1 oz) portion of chicken bouillon made up
in a jug with (225 ml or 8 fl oz) of boiling water
300 ml (½ pint) double cream
Salt to taste

1 Sauté onions in butter until soft.

2 Add garlic and spices and cook for a few minutes.

3 Add diced chicken and cook for about 5 minutes.

4 Add tomatoes, sugar, chicken bouillon and simmer for about 30 minutes.

5 Remove from heat and, just before serving, add cream.

6 Season to taste.

CORONATION CHICKEN

 Coronation Chicken is time-consuming to make. I would purchase Coronation-flavoured mayonnaise and mix it with freshly cooked, chopped chicken breast.

This is a quick recipe which you could try if you want to make your own Coronation Chicken.

---

250 g (9 oz) onion, chopped
A little vegetable oil
1 litre (2 pints) mayonnaise
2 heaped tsp tomato purée
2 heaped tbs curry powder or paste
1 tbs lemon juice
4 tbs mango chutney
225 ml (8 fl oz) double cream
Salt and pepper to taste

---

1 Gently fry onions in oil and leave to cool.

2 Mix together mayonnaise, tomato purée, curry powder and lemon juice

3 Add mango chutney and mix well.

4 Add double cream and season to taste.

5 If required, add more curry powder and a little more mango chutney.

Fillings for sandwiches

There are endless varieties of fillings for sandwiches, wraps and paninis and I have listed below a few suggestions.

List on your menu several everyday varieties of sandwiches, wraps and paninis and a few of the more unusual ones. Or you could ask your customers to design their own sandwich. You could fix a price for a basic sandwich or wrap and then add an extra amount for each additional item they choose. For example, Cheese, Ham and Tomato would be £1.75 for a plain cheese sandwich or wrap, plus 50p for the ham and 30p for the tomato, making a total of £2.55 for that particular sandwich. You would obviously charge a bit more for a more expensive filling than you would for a salad filling.

- ☐ Chicken mayonnaise
- ☐ Prawn Marie Rose
- ☐ Prawn in sweet chilli and lime sauce
- ☐ Ham, cheese and tomato
- ☐ Hot roast beef with horseradish sauce
- ☐ Corned beef, tomato and spring onion with mayonnaise
- ☐ Barbeque chicken with mayonnaise and caramelized onions
- ☐ Cream cheese or cottage cheese with crispy bacon pieces

VEGETARIAN OPTIONS

- ☐ Cheese and apple coleslaw
- ☐ Brie, tomato and mayonnaise
- ☐ Avocado and Brie
- ☐ Egg mayonnaise
- ☐ Cheese and tomato
- ☐ Cheese and pickle
- ☐ Carrots, green pepper and cream cheese

TOASTED SANDWICHES AND PANINIS

☐ Cheese and ham

☐ Cheese, ham and pineapple

☐ Chicken, cheese and caramelized onion

☐ Chicken, cranberry sauce and mayonnaise

☐ Chicken, sweetcorn and mayonnaise

☐ Bacon, Brie and cranberry sauce with mayonnaise

☐ Bacon, Brie, tomato and mayonnaise

☐ Ham, roast peppers and cream cheese

☐ Smoked salmon and cream cheese

☐ Cheese, caramelized onion and mayonnaise

☐ Cheese and onion

☐ Brie, tomato and onion

☐ Cheese and pickle

☐ Cream cheese, roast peppers and onion

Serve all of the above with a salad garnish and a few crisps.

You can purchase plain or flavoured mayonnaise – for example, Tikka and Coronation mayonnaise – already made up in 5 or 10 litre tubs from most suppliers.

Popular cake and traybake recipes

SWEET SHORTCRUST PASTRY

500 g (1 lb 2 oz) plain flour
275 g (10 oz) Stork margarine
1 egg
50 ml (2 fl oz) cold water
150 g (5 oz) caster sugar

 Sift flour into a bowl.

❷ Cut the margarine into cubes and then rub it into the flour with your fingertips until the mixture resembles coarse breadcrumbs.

❸ Mix the egg, water and sugar with a whisk and then gradually add enough of the liquid to bind the dough.

❹ Gather into a ball, wrap in clingfilm and put into the fridge for about 20 minutes.

❺ On a lightly floured surface, roll out the dough to the shape of the flan dish or baking tray.

 You can use this pastry for pies and other recipes that require a pastry base.

 You can purchase tubs of ready-to-use chilled rhubarb and chilled Bramley apple pie filling from Baco. (See the useful contacts section in Appendix 7.)

COCONUT SLICE
1 recipe sweet shortcrust pastry (see page 142)

For the filling
300 g (11 oz) coconut
150 ml (¼ pint) hot milk
225 g (8 oz) margarine
225 g (8 oz) caster sugar
75 g (3 oz) rice flour
3 whole eggs and 1 egg white
Approx 450 g (1 lb) raspberry jam
A little melted chocolate

---

1 Soak the coconut in the hot milk.

2 Cream the margarine and sugar together.

3 Mix in the rice flour, add the eggs and beat well.

4 Add the softened coconut and mix well.

5 Use sweet shortcrust pastry to line the base of a baking tray measuring 34 cm x 23 cm (13½ in x 9 in) and cover with a layer of raspberry jam.*

6 Top with the coconut mixture and bake at 190°C (375°F), Gas Mark 5 for 45 mins or until golden.

7 When cool, drizzle with melted chocolate.

Note: I use seedless raspberry jam which is available in large jars from Tesco.

* (You probably won't need to use all the jam.)

OVEN SCONES

500 g (1 lb 2 oz) self-raising flour
4 heaped tsp baking powder
125 g (4 oz) caster sugar
2 eggs
200 ml (7 fl oz) milk
100 ml (3½ fl oz) vegetable oil

1 Sift together the flour and baking powder and then add the caster sugar.

2 Whisk the eggs, milk and vegetable oil together and pour into the dry ingredients.

3 Mix with a fork to form a soft dough.

4 Roll out on a lightly floured surface and cut into rounds about 2½ – 3 cm (1 – 1¼ in) thick with an 8 cm (3 in) cutter.

5 Bake on a non-stick baking sheet at 200°C (400°F), Gas Mark 6 for 10 – 12 minutes or until golden.

You can increase or decrease the size of the scones if you want to.

Variations For fruit scones just add 150 g (5 oz) sultanas or dried fruit to the mix before adding the liquid to the dry ingredients. You can try crystallized ginger, dates, cranberries or cheese for a change.

For jam and cream scones, cool the scones, split them open and spread strawberry jam on one side and whipped double cream on the other, then sandwich them together. These are delicious and sell very well.

CARROT CAKE

For the cake
450 ml (¾ pint) vegetable oil
8 eggs
450 g (1 lb) caster sugar
2 tsp vanilla flavouring
450 g plain flour
15 g (½ oz) bicarbonate of soda
15 g (½ oz) baking powder
20 g (¾ oz) cinnamon
15 g (½ oz) salt
5 g (⅛ oz) mixed spice

625 g (1 lb 6 oz) carrots, grated
150 g (5 oz) walnut pieces, chopped quite small

To make the cake

1 Mix oil, eggs, sugar and vanilla flavouring.

2 Sieve all dry ingredients.

3 Add dry ingredients to oil, eggs, sugar and vanilla flavouring and mix.

4 Add grated carrots and chopped walnuts and mix well.

5 Grease and line a 35 cm x 25 cm (14 in x 10 in) cake tin with non-stick baking paper.

6 Bake at 180°C (350°F), Gas Mark 4 for 45 mins – 1 hour (for a fan oven, reduce the temperature to 170°C).

If you like a spicier cake you can add more mixed spice and cinnamon.

 I always use Tesco unbleached non-stick Baking paper for lining all the baking trays.

I usually ice half of the cake to sell in the coffee shop and wrap the other half of the cake in tin foil to use the following day. Alternatively, you can freeze the other half if you don't think you will use it within three or four days. This cake keeps for up to four days in a sealed container.

For the cream cheese icing
125 g (4 oz) soft margarine or butter
250 g (9 oz) cream cheese
500 g (1 lb 2 oz) icing sugar
1 tsp vanilla flavouring

To make the icing

1 Cream the margarine and cream cheese together.

2 Add the vanilla flavouring and enough icing sugar to make a thick topping for the cake. If the icing is too stiff add a little water and mix until you are happy with the consistency. If the icing is too thin then add more icing sugar.

FRUIT LOAF

1½ cups (225 g or 8 oz) sultanas or mixed dried fruit
1 tsp mixed spice
1 tsp bicarbonate of soda
1 cup (125 g or 4 oz) sugar
225 g (8 oz) margarine
1 cup (300 ml or ½ pint) water
1 cup (125 g or 4 oz) self-raising flour
1 cup (125 g or 4 oz) plain flour
2 eggs

---

1 Put the sultanas, mixed spice, bicarbonate of soda, sugar, margarine and water into a pot and bring to the boil for one minute.

2 Cool and add the flour and eggs and mix thoroughly.

3 Put the mixture into a greased and lined 900 g (2lb) loaf tin.

4 Bake at 180°C (350°F), Gas Mark 4 for 1 – 1 ¼ hours.

5 Test with a cake tester or toothpick and if it comes out clean the cake is ready.

CRANBERRY NUT LOAF

---

120 ml (4 fl oz) vegetable oil
200 g (7 oz) soft brown or muscovado sugar
2 eggs, beaten
3 very ripe bananas, mashed
290 g (11 oz) self-raising flour
½ tsp baking powder
1 tsp baking soda
½ tsp salt
3 tbs milk
1 tsp vanilla flavouring
115 g (4 ½ oz) chopped walnuts
150 g (5 oz) dried cranberries

---

1 Beat the oil and sugar together.

2 Add the eggs and mashed bananas and beat well.

3 Add the sifted dry ingredients, milk and vanilla flavouring.

4 Mix well and stir in the nuts and cranberries.

5 Pour mixture into a greased and lined 700 g (1½ lb) loaf tin.

6 Bake for 1 hour to 1 hour and 10 mins at 180°C (350°F), Gas Mark 4 or until a cake tester or toothpick comes out clean.

APPLE SPICE LOAF

This is a very easy recipe as it is all done in a food processor.

---

120 ml (4 fl oz) vegetable oil
2 large eggs
200 g (7 oz) soft brown or muscovado sugar
300 ml (½ pint) partly cooked apples or tinned apples, diced
215 g (7½ oz) self-raising flour
4 tsp cinnamon
2 tsp mixed spice
1 heaped tsp baking soda
½ tsp salt
115 g (4 oz) chopped walnuts

---

1 Put all the ingredients into a food processor and switch on for about 10 seconds.

2 Scrape down the bowl and put the machine on to pulse until all the ingredients are mixed thoroughly. Do not over process.

3 Scrape out the bowl and put the mixture into a lined 700 g (1½ lb) loaf tin and bake at 190°C (375°F), Gas Mark 5 for about 1 hour or until a cake tester or toothpick comes out clean when inserted into the centre of the loaf.

 You can purchase a tub of Bramley apples for using in cakes and pies from Baco (see the useful contacts section in Appendix 7). This will save you a lot of time peeling and slicing cooking apples.

APPLE SPICE CHOCOLATE CHIP CAKE

---

240 ml (8½ fl oz) vegetable oil
4 large eggs
400 g (14 oz) soft brown or muscovado sugar
600 ml (1 pint) partly cooked apples or tinned apples, diced
450 g (1 lb) self-raising flour
3 tsp baking soda
1 tsp salt
8 tsp cinnamon
4 tsp mixed spice
200 g (7 oz) milk chocolate chips
100 g (4 oz) milk chocolate chips for decoration

---

1 Mix all the ingredients except the chocolate chips together in a food processor for about 15 seconds.

2 Scrape down the bowl and add 200 g chocolate chips. Put the machine on to pulse until the ingredients are mixed thoroughly. Do not over process.

3 Scrape the mixture into a lined cake tin 35 cm x 25 cm (14 in x 10 in) and bake in a preheated oven at 190°C (375°F), Gas Mark 5 for about 1 hour or until the cake tester or toothpick comes out clean when inserted into the centre of the cake.

4 When the cake is cool, ice with butter icing and sprinkle with chocolate chips.

If you want to make a smaller cake use half of the ingredients and bake in a lined 23 cm x 18 cm (9 in x 7 in) cake tin.

STICKY TOFFEE BUNS

---

85 g (3½ oz) butter
175 g (6 oz) soft brown or muscovado sugar
1 tsp mixed spice
1 tsp cinnamon
2 eggs beaten
175 g (6 oz) self-raising flour
250 ml (9 fl oz) tea
½ tsp bicarbonate of soda
250 g (9 oz) stoned dates, chopped

---

1 Cream the butter and sugar together.

2 Add the mixed spice and cinnamon.

3 Add the beaten egg and flour alternately.

4 Make the tea using one tea bag and 250 ml (9 fl oz) boiling water.

5 Remove the tea bag, pour the tea into a saucepan, add the bicarbonate of soda and dates then simmer for approximately 3 minutes or until the dates are soft.

6 Let the date mixture cool slightly before folding it into the butter, sugar and egg mixture.

7 Put the mixture into large muffin cases in a muffin tray and tray and bake in a pre-heated oven at 180°C (350°F), Gas Mark 4 for about 20 – 25 minutes.

8 To see if the buns are ready, insert a cake tester or toothpick into the middle of one and if it comes out clean the buns are ready.

9 When the buns are cool, ice them with caramel butter icing or, for a sticky topping, spread a little boiled, condensed milk over them.

For the caramel butter icing
100 g (4 oz) dark muscovado sugar
100 g (4 oz) butter
130 ml (4½ oz) double cream
1 tsp vanilla flavouring
300 g (11 oz) icing sugar, sifted

To make the caramel butter icing

1 Bring the sugar, butter and cream slowly to the boil.

2 Add the vanilla flavouring.

3 Remove from the heat and leave to cool.

4 Add the icing sugar and blend until the mixture is smooth.

5 Add a little more cream or a little more icing sugar until you reach the desired consistency.

Variation To serve as a dessert, you can top a sticky toffee bun with ice cream and sticky toffee sauce.

For the toffee sauce
100 g (4 oz) dark muscovado sugar
100 g (4 oz) butter
130 ml (4½ fl oz) double cream
1 tsp vanilla flavouring

To make the toffee sauce

1 Melt the sugar, butter and cream together.

2 Add the vanilla flavouring.

3 Simmer until the sauce is a nice toffee colour.

CUPCAKES

---

125 g (4 oz) butter or soft margarine
375 g (13 oz) caster sugar
1 tsp vanilla flavouring
4 eggs plus 2 yolks
315 g (11½ oz) self-raising flour or McDougall's supreme sponge flour
½ tsp salt
250 ml (9 fl oz) double cream

---

1 Cream the butter or margarine and sugar together until light and fluffy.

2 Add the vanilla flavouring.

3 Add the eggs and yolks one at a time, beating well after you add each one.

4 Add the sifted flour and the cream alternately, beginning and ending with the flour.

5 Put the mixture into large muffin cases in a muffin tin.

6 Bake in a preheated oven at 180°C (350°F), Gas Mark 4 for 15 to 20 minutes or until the tops are golden and a cake tester inserted into the centre comes out clean.

7 When cool, ice with coloured butter icing, e.g. pink, lemon, blue.

Variations You can decorate the cupcakes with sugar strands, Smarties or miniature chocolate easter eggs. Children love these cakes, especially if they are brightly decorated.

You can also use this recipe to make butterfly cakes.

To make butterfly cakes

1 Slice the top off each cake and cut this slice in half.

2 Pipe a swirl of whipped double cream in the centre of each cake.

3 Place the half slices of cake into the cream at an angle to resemble butterfly wings.

4 Dust the cake with icing sugar.

If you don't want to use double cream you can use butter icing.

To make butter icing
200 g (7 oz) butter or margarine, softened
700 g (1 lb 8 oz) icing sugar, sifted

---

1 Mix ingredients together until you get a creamy consistency.

GINGERBREAD

*It took me over a year to get a really good gingerbread recipe
and this one is delicious every time.*

---

450 g (1 lb) soft margarine or butter
450 g (1 lb) light soft brown or light muscovado sugar
350 g (12 oz) golden syrup
100 g (4 oz) treacle
700 g (1 lb 8 oz) plain flour
8 level tsp ground ginger
4 level tsp mixed spice
4 eggs, beaten
4 level tsp bicarbonate of soda
600 ml (1 pint) milk, warmed

---

❶ Melt the margarine or butter, brown sugar, syrup and treacle together in a pot.

❷ Sift the flour and spices together then stir into the melted mixture along with the beaten eggs.

❸ Add the bicarbonate of soda to the warm milk and stir to mix thoroughly.

❹ Slowly add the warm milk and bicarbonate of soda to the mixture in the pot and stir well to make sure all the flour is free of lumps.

❺ Pour into a lined cake tin 35 cm x 25 cm (14 in x 10 in) and bake in a preheated oven at 150°C (300°F), Gas Mark 2 for 45 min, then cover the top with a sheet of greaseproof paper for the final 15 min.

❻ The gingerbread is ready when a cake tester inserted into the centre comes out clean.

Ice with a thick icing made from icing sugar and a little water.

I usually use half the cake and wrap the other half in tin foil to use in the next couple of days. This cake will keep well in a sealed container for three days. The gingerbread can also be frozen.

PLAIN SPONGE

If you want to make a very light sponge then use McDougall's supreme sponge flour.
It works out more expensive but it is really very good.

---

450 g (1 lb) caster sugar
450 g (1 lb) soft margarine or butter
8 eggs
550 g (1 lb 4 oz) self-raising flour
4 tsp baking powder
7 tablespoons milk
1 tbs vanilla flavouring

---

1 Cream the sugar and margarine or butter until light and fluffy and then beat the eggs in one at a time.

2 Fold in the sieved flour and baking powder alternately with the milk.

3 Add the vanilla flavouring.

4 Pour into a lined baking tin 35 cm x 25 cm (14 in x 10 in) and bake in a preheated oven at 180°C (350°F), Gas Mark 4 for 45 – 50 minutes.

 You can use half the mixture to make a small sponge in a 23 cm x 18 cm (9 in x 7 in) cake tin or you can use the mixture to make cupcakes.

Variations Instead of vanilla flavouring use the juice and rind of 2 lemons and make lemon-flavoured water icing for the top.

Omit the vanilla flavouring and add 200 g (7oz) dark Belgian chocolate, melted, to make a chocolate cake. Top with chocolate butter icing and sprinkle with grated chocolate.

When the sponge has cooled, split it in half and spread raspberry or strawberry jam over one half and whipped double cream over the other half. Then sandwich the two halves together and dust the top with icing sugar.

QUICK AND EASY SHORTBREAD

This is a very easy recipe and the shortbread sells well in our coffee shop. Always use butter
for shortbread as there is a difference in the taste if you use margarine.

---

450 g (1 lb) butter
225 g (8 oz) sugar
675 g (1 lb 8 oz) plain flour

---

1 Cream the butter and sugar together.

2 Add the sieved flour and mix well but do not over mix.

3 Roll out on a lightly floured surface and cut with a large fluted cutter to the size you require. Place on a tray lined with non-stick baking paper.

4 Prick the shortbread all over with a fork and bake at 160°C (325°F), Gas Mark 3 in a preheated oven until shortbread is a pale golden colour.

5 Remove shortbread from the oven and immediately dust them with caster sugar.

 If the mixture is too soft add a little more flour until it begins to bind together.

FINE SHORTBREAD

---

225 g (8 oz) butter
100 g (4 oz) caster sugar
450 g (1 lb) plain flour
100 g (4 oz) cornflour

---

1 Cream the butter and sugar together.

2 Sift the flour and cornflour together then add them to the butter and sugar mixture.

3 Knead the mixture lightly it until it forms a dough.

4 Roll out on a lightly floured surface. Cut out large fluted shapes to the size you require and place on a tray lined with non-stick baking paper.

5 Prick the shortbread all over with a fork and bake in a preheated oven at 160°C (325°F), Gas Mark 3 for about 30 minutes or until they are a light golden colour.

6 Immediately you take them out of the oven, sprinkle caster sugar all over them.

EMPIRE BISCUITS

This is the recipe we use in our coffee shop and these biscuits sell very well.

450 g (1 lb) plain flour
225 g (8 oz) icing sugar
225 g (8 oz) cornflour
450 g (1 lb) soft margarine

1 Sift all the dry ingredients together.

2 Mix in the margarine until the mixture forms a dough.

3 Roll out the dough on a lightly floured surface and cut out shapes with a large cutter the size of the required biscuit. Place on a tray lined with non-stick baking paper.

4 Bake in a preheated oven at 160°C (325°F), Gas Mark 3 for about 35 minutes or until biscuits are a very light golden colour.

5 Cool on a rack then sandwich together with seedless raspberry jam.

6 Ice the tops of the biscuits with icing and decorate with a cherry or coloured sugar strands.

Tray bakes

FUDGE SLICES

225 g (8 oz) margarine
1 large tin condensed milk
4 tbs golden syrup
500 g (1 lb 2 oz) digestive biscuits, crushed
300 g (11 oz) milk chocolate, melted

1 Melt margarine, condensed milk and syrup in a pan together and bring to the boil.

2 Boil for 4 minutes.

3 Remove from the heat and add the crushed digestive biscuits and mix quickly.

4 Press into a Swiss roll tin.

5 Cover with melted chocolate.

Instead of making the caramel in steps 1 and 2 you can melt luxury caramel purchased from Baco (see Appendix 7 for contact details).

RICH CHOCOLATE SHORTCAKE

125 g (4 oz) hard margarine
1 small tin condensed milk
275 g (10 oz) crushed shortbread crumbs
300 g (11 oz) Supercook Belgian milk chocolate
300 g (11 oz) Supercook Belgian white chocolate
50 g (2 oz) melted milk or plain chocolate for drizzling over the finished tray bake

1 Melt the milk chocolate.

2 Melt the margarine and add the melted chocolate and condensed milk.

3 Add the crushed shortbread crumbs to the mixture.

4 Press shortcake into a tray 20 cm x 30 cm (8 in x 12 in).

5 Leave to cool (not in the fridge)

6 Cover with melted white chocolate and leave to harden.

7 When the chocolate is hard, drizzle milk or plain chocolate over it.

8 Cut the shortcake into approximately 10 -12 slices.

Variation Instead of drizzling chocolate over the shortcake you can sprinkle it with milk chocolate chips immediately after covering the bake with melted white chocolate.

 When you are making shortbread, make extra and crush it for use in the above recipe. You can do this in advance and store it in an airtight container.

MARS BAR SQUARES

Most people know how to make this but I have included the recipe because it is always popular.

9 Mars bars
225 g (8 oz) hard margarine
1 tbs golden syrup
8 – 9 mugs of Rice Krispies
600 g (1 lb 5 oz) melted Scotbloc cake cover or Belgian milk chocolate

1 Melt the Mars bars, syrup and margarine together.

2 Remove from heat and immediately mix in the Rice Krispies.

3 Spread the mixture over a large tray approximately 30 cm x 40 cm (12 in x 16 in).

4 Leave to cool then cover with melted chocolate.

5 Leave to set and cut into approximately 20 – 24 squares.

MILLIONAIRE SHORTBREAD

For the shortbread base
225 g (8 oz) caster sugar
450 g (1 lb) butter or margarine
675 g (1 lb 8 oz) plain flour

---

1 Cream the sugar and butter together.

2 Add the flour and mix until a dough forms.

3 Press into a large tray measuring 34 cm x 24 cm (13½ in x 9½ in).

4 Bake at 180°C (350°F), Gas Mark 4 until the shortbread is a light golden colour.

For the caramel
225 g (8 oz) margarine or butter
225 g (8 oz) golden caster sugar
1 large tin condensed milk
4 tbs golden syrup
300 g (11 oz) milk Scotbloc

---

1 Melt the margarine, sugar, condensed milk and syrup in a saucepan.

2 Boil slowly for 5 minutes, stirring continuously.

3 Pour the mixture over the cooled shortbread base.

4 When the caramel is cool, cover with melted Scotbloc.

Variation For a change, use white Supercook Scotbloc to cover the caramel shortbread.

If you haven't time to make the caramel filling for Millionaire Shortbread and Crispy Surprise (on page 158) you can purchase a large tub of luxury caramel from Baco (see Appendix 7 for contact details) and melt it slightly to use on the shortbread base. This is more convenient and less time-consuming if you are going to make quite a lot of tray bakes.

I use the Millionaire Shortbread mixture to make tart cases for Strawberry Tart and Toffee Tart.

To make the tart cases

❶ Line greased tart tins with the shortbread mixture.

❷ Bake in a preheated oven at 180°C (350°F), Gas Mark 4 until golden.

❸ Leave to cool.

To make the Strawberry Tarts

❶ Fill the tarts with whipped double cream and slices of fresh strawberries.

❷ Cover with raspberry or strawberry jelly (tubs are obtainable from your major supplier).

To make the Toffee Tarts

❶ Fill the tart cases with ready-boiled condensed milk (available from the supermarket).

❷ Drizzle with melted chocolate.

CRISPY SURPRISE

Make a base in a lined Swiss roll tin 20 cm x 30 cm (8 in x 12 in) using the shortbread mixture above.

For the caramel
225 g (8 oz) margarine or butter
225 g (8 oz) golden caster sugar
1 large tin condensed milk
4 tbs golden syrup

---

❶ Melt the margarine or butter, sugar, condensed milk and syrup in a pan.

❷ Boil slowly for 5 minutes, stirring continuously

❸ Pour the mixture over the cooled shortbread base.

For the topping
200 g (7 oz) dessicated coconut
1 large tin condensed milk
250 g (9 oz) chocolate
125 g (4 oz) Rice Krispies

---

1 Mix the desiccated coconut with the condensed milk.

2 Spread over the caramel base.

3 Mix the melted chocolate and Rice Krispies and spread on top of the coconut layer.

4 Allow to cool and cut into 12 pieces.

I use Belgian chocolate for a better flavour, but you can use Scotbloc for a less expensive recipe.

 TIP I would have some muffin cases ready and put the remainder of the chocolate crispy mix into them to make individual crispy cakes. This saves any waste.

BANOFFEE PIE

---

100 g (4 oz) butter or margarine
225 g (8 oz) digestive biscuits, crushed
1 can condensed milk, boiled (or a ready-boiled can of condensed milk)
2 bananas
300 ml (½ pint) double cream
2 plain chocolate, grated

---

1 Grease a 25 cm (10 in) flan dish.

2 Melt the butter in the microwave, add the crushed digestive biscuits and mix well.

3 Press the biscuit mixture into the flan dish and put into the fridge for 30 minutes.

4 Open the cooled can of caramel and spread over the biscuit base.

5 Slice the bananas and place on top of the caramel.

6 Whisk the cream and spread it over the bananas.

7 Sprinkle with grated chocolate or vermicelli to finish.

 **TIP** You can make your own caramel filling by covering cans of condensed milk with hot water and boiling for 3 hours. Always keep the cans covered with water and do not allow them to boil dry. You can boil several cans at a time and they will keep for a few weeks unopened.

STRAWBERRY AND VANILLA CHEESECAKE

---

225 g (8 oz) digestive biscuits, crushed
100 g (4 oz) butter
350 g (12 oz) full fat cream cheese
75 g (3 oz) caster sugar
2 eggs, separated
1 tsp vanilla flavouring
1 tsp gelatine
300 ml (½ pint) whipping cream
A few strawberries to decorate

---

1 Grease a 25 cm (10 in) flan dish.

2 Melt the butter in the microwave, add the crushed digestive biscuits and mix well.

3 Press the biscuit mixture into the flan dish and put into the fridge for 30 minutes.

4 Put the cream cheese and sugar in a bowl and mix together until the cheese softens.

5 Stir in the egg yolks and vanilla flavouring.

6 Mix the gelatine with 2 tbs hot water in a small bowl and stand the bowl in a pan of hot water until the gelatine is clear.

7 Whip the cream until it forms soft peaks.

8 Whisk the egg whites in a clean, dry bowl until they peak softly.

9 Once the gelatine has cooled slightly beat it into the cheese mixture and fold in ½ of the cream.

10 Spread the mixture over the biscuit base.

11 Chill in the fridge until the mixture has set.

12 Pipe the remaining cream onto the top of the cheesecake and decorate with halves of strawberries.

SCOTTISH TABLET

1 large can condensed milk
100 g (4 oz) butter
1 cup (225 ml or 8 fl oz) full cream milk
900 g (2 lb) granulated sugar
1tsp vanilla flavouring

1 Melt the butter in a heavy-based pot, add the milk and condensed milk and heat gently.

2 Add the sugar and when it has dissolved, bring the mixture to the boil and then turn down the heat to a fast simmer for approximately 20 minutes.

3 Stir continuously to prevent the mixture sticking to the bottom of the pan and burning. The colour will turn to light caramel.

4 To test the mixture, drop a teaspoon of it into a cup of ice-cold water and leave it for about 15 seconds. If you can roll it into a soft ball the mixture is ready. If it is not ready, simmer for a few more minutes and test it again.

5 Remove the mixture from the heat and add the vanilla flavouring.

6 Beat the mixture rapidly with a wooden spoon until you feel it getting grainy.

7 Pour mixture into a greased, lined tin 20 cm x 30 cm (8 in x 12 in).

8 Leave to cool and cut into 12 slices or into smaller squares.

Variation You can omit the vanilla flavouring and add Bailey's Irish Cream, almond flavouring or any other flavouring you would like to try.

VANILLA FUDGE

---

300 ml (½ pint) full cream milk
225 g (8 oz) butter
900 g (2 lb) granulated sugar
2 tbs golden syrup
1 can condensed milk
1 tsp vanilla flavouring

---

1 Melt the butter, milk and condensed milk together and heat gently.

2 Add the sugar and allow it to dissolve.

3 Add the syrup and bring the mixture slowly to the boil.

4 Turn down the heat and simmer gently, stirring occasionally, for about 35 minutes.

5 To test the mixture, drop a teaspoon of it into a cup of ice-cold water, leave it for about 15 seconds and if you can then roll it into a soft ball it is ready.

6 Remove the mixture from the heat and leave to cool for 5 minutes.

7 Add the vanilla flavouring and beat the mixture vigorously with a wooden spoon until it is thick and grainy.

8 Pour quickly into a greased and lined tin 20 cm x 30 cm (8 in x 12 in).

9 When the fudge is cold cut it into squares.

Baco can supply you with most of the ingredients required for baking but they also supply Muffin Mix which is excellent – all you have to do is add whatever fruit etc. you wish; and Craig Millar Scone Mix – just add sultanas, cheese, dates, ginger, cranberries or whatever else you want in your oven scones. See Appendix 7 for contact details.

13
THE 12 SKILLS YOU NEED TO RUN A SUCCESSFUL COFFEE SHOP

Now that you have opened your coffee shop in a great location you will be wondering what it takes to run it successfully. I have listed below 12 essential skills that I think you must have in order to do this.

1. Keep your coffee shop spotlessly clean.

2. Offer good and interesting food at a reasonable price.

3. Give excellent customer service.

4. Have good communication skills.

5. Be friendly and approachable; talk to your customers.

6. Be open to suggestions on how to improve your service.

7. Be a great boss.

8. Set a good example to your staff.

9. Be a skilful manager.

10. Develop problem-solving skills.

11. Try to keep calm under all circumstances.

12. Be able to evaluate your progress and set feasible goals for the future.

I wish you every success in your new venture.

APPENDIX 1
EMPLOYMENT CONTRACT: FULL-TIME STAFF

(This is a copy of the contract document which I used in my coffee shop.)

ANOTHER COFFEE SHOP LTD

STATEMENT OF PARTICULARS OF EMPLOYMENT

COFFEE SHOP: FULL-TIME NEW EMPLOYEES

This Statement dated ....……........ sets out the main terms of your employment with **Another Coffee Shop Ltd, 125 Broccoli Street, Glasgow G21 9AB** which the Company is required to provide to you under the Employment Rights Act 1996. This Statement together with your offer letter and the Employee Handbook form your written contract of employment.

Employee: ....

Employee Handbook:
The Employee Handbook is available for you to consult in the Office.

Commencement of Employment:
Your employment with the Company commenced on....................

Job Title:
The title of the job which you are employed to do is ....

The Company may amend your duties from time to time and may require you to undertake other duties as necessary to meet the needs of the business.

Probationary Period:
Your employment is subject to satisfactory completion of a three-month probationary period. The Company reserves the right to extend this period at its discretion.

The Company will assess and review your work performance during this time and reserves the right to terminate your employment at any time during the probationary period.

During the first month of your probationary period, either the Company or you may give one day's notice to terminate your employment. After one month's service and up to satisfactory completion of your probationary period, the Company or you may terminate your employment by giving one week's notice.

Place of Work:

Your usual place of work is ………………………………………………………………………..

Pay:

Your rate of pay is £……………… per hour, payable weekly on a Friday by credit transfer, in arrears.

Deductions:

The Company reserves the right to deduct any outstanding monies you owe to the Company from your pay or, on termination of employment, from your final pay. This includes any previous error or overpayment, holiday or time off in lieu taken but not yet accrued, the costs of cash shortages from the till, and the cost of personal calls on Company telephones.

Hours of Work:

Your working week will comprise 20 hours between the hours of 10 a.m. and 6 p.m. The hours you are required to work will vary depending on the needs of the business and will be organized according to a rota, which you will be notified of on a weekly basis.

You are entitled to a daily half hour paid meal break.

The Company may require you to perform a reasonable amount of work outside your normal hours of work, depending on the needs of the business. You are entitled to receive payment for this work at your normal rate of pay.

Short-Time Working and Lay-Off:

The Company reserves the right to introduce short-time working or a period of temporary lay-off without pay where this is necessary to avoid redundancies or where there is a shortage of work. The Company will comply with any statutory guaranteed minimum payment obligations.

Statutory Rights in Relation to Sunday Shop Work:

You have become employed as a shop worker and are or can be required under your contract of employment to do the Sunday work your contract provides for.

However, if you wish, you can give a notice, as described in the next paragraph, to your employer and you will then have the right not to work in or about a shop on any Sunday on which the shop is open once three months have passed from the date on which you gave the notice.

Your notice must:

☐ be in writing;

☐ be signed and dated by you;

☐ say that you object to Sunday working.

For three months after you give the notice, your employer can still require you to do all the Sunday work your contract provides for. After the three-month period has ended, you have the right to complain to an employment tribunal if, because of your refusal to work on Sundays on which the shop is open, your employer:

☐ dismisses you; or

☐ does something else detrimental to you, for example, failing to promote you.

Once you have the rights described, you can surrender them only by giving your employer a further notice, signed and dated by you, saying that you wish to work on Sunday or that you do not object to Sunday working and then agreeing with your employer to work on Sundays or on a particular Sunday.

Annual Holidays:

The holiday year runs from 1st January to 31st December.

Your annual holiday entitlement in any holiday year is four weeks excluding all public holidays.

Holiday Entitlement:

Annual holiday entitlement accrues at the rate of one twelfth of the full annual holiday entitlement, on the 1st of each month, in advance during the first year of employment.

You will be paid at the normal rate of pay in respect of periods of annual holiday. Overtime will not normally be included in the calculation of holiday pay, except where the overtime is contractually guaranteed.

In the event of termination of employment, you will be entitled to holiday pay calculated on a pro-rata basis in respect of all annual holiday already accrued but not taken at the date of termination of employment.

If, on termination of employment, you have taken more annual holiday entitlement than you have accrued in that holiday year, an appropriate deduction will be made from your final payment.

Public Holidays:

Full-time employees are entitled to four public holidays each year, and will be advised of the relevant dates as early as possible. The public holidays that are recognized are:

....

Where the coffee shop closes on a public holiday and the employee has exhausted his or her pro rata public holiday entitlement, the employee will not be paid for this day. If the employee wishes to be paid for this day, he or she should take this time from his or her annual holiday entitlement, or arrange to work on an alternative day, at the sole discretion of the Company in accordance with the needs of the business.

Where a recognized public holiday falls on a Saturday or a Sunday, alternative dates will not be substituted for these. Employees will be advised of these as early as possible.

Sick Pay:
If you are absent from work because of sickness or injury you will be entitled to Statutory Sick Pay, provided you meet the qualifying conditions.

Absence Reporting:
You are required to notify the Company as soon as possible of your sickness absence and the reasons for it. You should do this personally at the earliest opportunity to the coffee shop owner, no later than 10 a.m. on the first day of your absence.

Notice:

Following successful completion of your probationary period, you are required to give two weeks' notice in writing to terminate your employment with the Company.

Following successful completion of your probationary period, you are entitled to receive the following written notice of termination of employment from the Company:

End of probationary period but less than
two years' continuous service: One week.

Two years' continuous service or longer: One week for each complete
                                                  year of service up to a maximum
                                                  of 12 weeks after 12 years' service.

The Company may exclude these notice provisions in the event of dismissal for gross misconduct.

The Company reserves the right to make payment in lieu of notice.

Disciplinary and Dismissal Appeals:

If you are dissatisfied with any disciplinary or dismissal decision taken in respect of you, you have the right of appeal.

Grievance Procedure:

Your employer encourages all employees to settle grievances informally. If, however, you have a grievance relating to any aspect of your employment which you would like to be resolved formally, you must set out the grievance and the basis for it in writing and submit it to the coffee shop owner.

Post-Termination Grievance:

Should you wish to raise a grievance after your employment has ended, you should submit the grievance in writing to the coffee shop owner.

Dress and Appearance:

You are required to dress smartly during working hours and to wear any Company clothing which has been supplied to you. Should you turn up for work dressed inappropriately, the Company reserves the right to send you home.

UNIFORMS:

It is a condition of your employment that you wear a uniform at all times during your working hours.

The Company will supply you with the necessary uniform at the Company's expense. You are expected to take care of this and to maintain it in a reasonable condition.

You are required to return your uniform in reasonable condition upon termination of your employment.

Health and Safety:

You are required to gain an understanding of the Company's health and safety procedures, observe them, and ensure that safety equipment and clothing are always used. The Company's health and safety information is displayed on the Coffee Shop notice board.

Staff Discount:

The Coffee Shop operates a staff discount scheme which you are entitled to take advantage of. Full details of the scheme are available from the coffee shop manager.

Changes to Terms of Employment:

The Company reserves the right to make reasonable changes to any of your terms and conditions of employment and will notify you in writing of such changes at the earliest opportunity and, in any event, within one month of such changes taking effect.

Declaration:

I understand that during the course of my employment it will be necessary for the Company to maintain personnel records in relation to my employment. Any information held concerning my employment which is personal data and which is processed by the Company for these purposes shall be processed only in accordance with the Data Protection Act 1998.

Acknowledgement:

I acknowledge receipt of this Statement. I have been shown the Employee Handbook. I confirm that I have read the Statement and the Employee Handbook which set out the principal rules, policies and procedures relating to my employment and which together with my offer letter form my written contract of employment.

Signed by the employee. ....

Date..

Signed for and on behalf of **ANOTHER COFFEE SHOP LTD**

....

Date..

APPENDIX 2
EMPLOYMENT CONTRACT: PART-TIME STAFF

(This is a copy of the contract document which I used in my coffee shop.)

ANOTHER COFFEE SHOP LTD

STATEMENT OF PARTICULARS OF EMPLOYMENT

COFFEE SHOP: PART-TIME NEW EMPLOYEES

This Statement dated ....………… sets out the main terms of your employment with **Another Coffee Shop Ltd, 125 Broccoli Street, Glasgow G21 9AB** which the Company is required to provide to you under the Employment Rights Act 1996. This Statement together with your offer letter and the Employee Handbook form your written contract of employment.

Employee: …………………………………..

Employee Handbook:

The Employee Handbook is available for you to consult in the Office.

Commencement of Employment:

Your employment with the Company commenced on…………………

Job Title:

The title of the job which you are employed to do is ……………………………….

The Company may amend your duties from time to time and may require you to undertake other duties as necessary to meet the needs of the business.

Probationary Period:

Your employment is subject to satisfactory completion of a three-month probationary period. The Company reserves the right to extend this period at its discretion.

The Company will assess and review your work performance during this time and reserves the right to terminate your employment at any time during the probationary period.

During the first month of your probationary period, either the Company or you may give one day's notice to terminate your employment. After one month's service and up to satisfactory completion of your probationary period, the Company or you may terminate your employment by giving one week's notice.

Place of Work:

Your usual place of work is ……………………………………………………………………..

Pay:

Your rate of pay is £……………… per hour, payable weekly on a Friday by credit transfer, in arrears.

Deductions:

The Company reserves the right to deduct any outstanding monies you owe to the Company from your pay or, on termination of employment, from your final pay. This includes any previous error or overpayment, holiday or time off in lieu taken but not yet accrued, the costs of cash shortages from the till, and the cost of personal calls on Company telephones.

Hours of Work:

Your working hours are on a part-time basis between the hours of 10 a.m. and 6 p.m. The hours you are required to work will vary depending on the needs of the business and will be organized according to a rota, which you will be notified of on a weekly basis.

You are entitled to the statutory minimum rest breaks according to the hours you work as set out in the current regulations.

Short-Time Working and Lay-Off:

The Company reserves the right to introduce short-time working or a period of temporary lay-off without pay where this is necessary to avoid redundancies or where there is a shortage of work.   The Company will comply with any statutory guaranteed minimum payment obligations.

Statutory Rights in Relation to Sunday Shop Work:

You have become employed as a shop worker and are or can be required under your contract of employment to do the Sunday work your contract provides for.

However, if you wish, you can give a notice, as described in the next paragraph, to your employer and you will then have the right not to work in or about a shop on any Sunday on which the shop is open once three months have passed from the date on which you gave the notice.

Your notice must:

☐ be in writing;

☐ be signed and dated by you;

☐ say that you object to Sunday working.

For three months after you give the notice, your employer can still require you to do all the Sunday work your contract provides for. After the three-month period has ended, you have the right to complain to an employment tribunal if, because of your refusal to work on Sundays on which the shop is open, your employer:

☐ dismisses you; or

☐ does something else detrimental to you, for example, failing to promote you.

Once you have the rights described, you can surrender them only by giving your employer a further notice, signed and dated by you, saying that you wish to work on Sunday or that you do not object to Sunday working and then agreeing with your employer to work on Sundays or on a particular Sunday.

Annual Holidays:

The holiday year runs from 1st January to 31st December.

Your annual holiday entitlement in any holiday year is four weeks excluding all public holiday entitlement.

Annual holiday entitlement accrues at the rate of one twelfth of the full annual holiday entitlement, on the 1st of each month, in advance in the first year of employment.

Employees with no normal working hours will be paid their average pay in the 12 weeks prior to the holiday.

In the event of termination of employment, you will be entitled to holiday pay calculated on a pro-rata basis in respect of all annual holiday already accrued but not taken at the date of termination of employment.

If, on termination of employment, you have taken more annual holiday entitlement than you have accrued in that holiday year, an appropriate deduction will be made from your final payment.

Public Holidays:

Full-time employees are entitled to ....public holidays each year. Part-time employees are entitled to public holidays pro rata. Where the Coffee Shop closes on a public holiday and the employee has exhausted his or her pro rata public holiday entitlement, the employee will not be paid for this day. If the employee wishes to be paid for this day, he or she should take this time from his or her annual holiday entitlement, or arrange to work on an alternative day, at the sole discretion of the Company in accordance with the needs of the business.

Where a recognized public holiday falls on a Saturday or a Sunday, alternative dates will not be substituted for these. Employees will be advised of these as early as possible.

Sick Pay:

If you are absent from work because of sickness or injury you will be entitled to Statutory Sick Pay, provided you meet the qualifying conditions.

Absence Reporting:

You are required to notify the Company as soon as possible of your sickness absence and the reasons for it. You should do this personally at the earliest opportunity to the coffee shop owner, no later than 10 a.m. on the first day of your absence.

Notice:

Following successful completion of your probationary period, you are required to give two weeks' notice in writing to terminate your employment with the Company.

Following successful completion of your probationary period, you are entitled to receive the following written notice of termination of employment from the Company:

End of probationary period but less than
two years' continuous service: One week.

Two years' continuous service or longer: One week for each complete
                                              year of service up to a maximum
                                              of 12 weeks after 12 years' service.

The Company may exclude these notice provisions in the event of dismissal for gross misconduct.

The Company reserves the right to make payment in lieu of notice.

Disciplinary and Dismissal Appeals:

If you are dissatisfied with any disciplinary or dismissal decision taken in respect of you, you have the right of appeal.

Grievance Procedure:

Your employer encourages all employees to settle grievances informally. If, however, you have a grievance relating to any aspect of your employment which you would like to be resolved formally, you must set out the grievance and the basis for it in writing and submit it to the coffee shop owner.

Post-Termination Grievance:

Should you wish to raise a grievance after your employment has ended, you should submit the grievance in writing to the coffee shop owner.

Dress and Appearance:

You are required to dress smartly during working hours and to wear any Company clothing which has been supplied to you. Should you turn up for work dressed inappropriately, the Company reserves the right to send you home.

UNIFORMS:

It is a condition of your employment that you wear a uniform at all times during your working hours.

The Company will supply you with the necessary uniform at the Company's expense. You are expected to take care of this and to maintain it in a reasonable condition.

You are required to return your uniform in reasonable condition upon termination of your employment.

Health and Safety:

You are required to gain an understanding of the Company's health and safety procedures, observe them, and ensure that safety equipment and clothing are always used. The Company's health and safety information is displayed on the Coffee Shop notice board.

Staff Discount:

The Coffee Shop operates a staff discount scheme which you are entitled to take advantage of. Full details of the scheme are available from the coffee shop manager.

Changes to Terms of Employment:

The Company reserves the right to make reasonable changes to any of your terms and conditions of employment and will notify you in writing of such changes at the earliest opportunity and, in any event, within one month of such changes taking effect.

Declaration:

I understand that during the course of my employment it will be necessary for the Company to maintain personnel records in relation to my employment. Any information held concerning my employment which is personal data and which is processed by the Company for these purposes shall be processed only in accordance with the Data Protection Act 1998.

Acknowledgement:

I acknowledge receipt of this Statement. I have been shown the Employee Handbook. I confirm that I have read the Statement and the Employee Handbook which set out the principal rules, policies and procedures relating to my employment and which together with my offer letter form my written contract of employment.

Signed by the employee ....

Date...

Signed for and on behalf of **ANOTHER COFFEE SHOP LTD**

....

Date...

APPENDIX 3
EMPLOYMENT CONTRACT: WEEKEND STAFF

(This is a copy of the contract document which I used in my coffee shop.)

ANOTHER COFFEE SHOP LTD

STATEMENT OF PARTICULARS OF EMPLOYMENT

COFFEE SHOP: WEEKEND NEW EMPLOYEES

This Statement dated ....………. sets out the main terms of your employment with **Another Coffee Shop Ltd, 125 Broccoli Street, Glasgow G21 9AB** which the Company is required to provide to you under the Employment Rights Act 1996. This Statement together with your offer letter and the Employee Handbook form your written contract of employment.

Employee: ………………………………..

Employee Handbook:
The Employee Handbook is available for you to consult in the Office.

Commencement of Employment:
Your employment with the Company commenced on…………………

Job Title:
The title of the job which you are employed to do is …………………………….
The Company may amend your duties from time to time and may require you to undertake other duties as necessary to meet the needs of the business.

Probationary Period:
Your employment is subject to satisfactory completion of a three-month probationary period. The Company reserves the right to extend this period at its discretion.

The Company will assess and review your work performance during this time and reserves the right to terminate your employment at any time during the probationary period.

During the first month of your probationary period, either the Company or you may give one day's notice to terminate your employment. After one month's service and up to satisfactory completion of your probationary period, the Company or you may terminate your employment by giving one week's notice.

Place of Work:

Your usual place of work is ……………………………………………………………..

Pay:

Your rate of pay is £……………… per hour, payable weekly on a Friday by credit transfer, in arrears.

Deductions:

The Company reserves the right to deduct any outstanding monies you owe to the Company from your pay or, on termination of employment, from your final pay. This includes any previous error or overpayment, holiday or time off in lieu taken but not yet accrued, the costs of cash shortages from the till, and the cost of personal calls on Company telephones.

Hours of Work:

Your hours of work are from 10 a.m. to 6 p.m. on a Saturday and from 12 noon to 5 p.m. on a Sunday.

You are entitled to a daily half hour paid meal break.

The Company may require you to perform a reasonable amount of work outside your normal hours of work, depending on the needs of the business. You are entitled to receive payment for this work at your normal rate of pay.

Short-Time Working and Lay-Off:

The Company reserves the right to introduce short-time working or a period of temporary lay-off without pay where this is necessary to avoid redundancies or where there is a shortage of work. The Company will comply with any statutory guaranteed minimum payment obligations.

Statutory Rights in Relation to Sunday Shop Work:

You have become employed as a shop worker and are or can be required under your contract of employment to do the Sunday work your contract provides for.

However, if you wish, you can give a notice, as described in the next paragraph, to your employer and you will then have the right not to work in or about a shop on any Sunday on which the shop is open once three months have passed from the date on which you gave the notice.

Your notice must:

☐ be in writing;

☐ be signed and dated by you;

☐ say that you object to Sunday working.

For three months after you give the notice, your employer can still require you to do all the Sunday work your contract provides for. After the three-month period has ended, you have the right to complain to an employment tribunal if, because of your refusal to work on Sundays on which the shop is open, your employer:

☐ dismisses you; or

☐ does something else detrimental to you, for example, failing to promote you.

Once you have the rights described, you can surrender them only by giving your employer a further notice, signed and dated by you, saying that you wish to work on Sunday or that you do not object to Sunday working and then agreeing with your employer to work on Sundays or on a particular Sunday.

Annual Holidays:

The holiday year runs from 1st January to 31st December.

Your annual holiday entitlement in any holiday year is four weeks excluding all public holiday entitlement.

Annual holiday entitlement accrues at the rate of one twelfth of the full annual holiday entitlement, on the 1st of each month, in advance.

Part-time, weekend employees' annual holiday entitlement accrues on a pro-rata basis.

You will be paid at their normal rate of pay in respect of periods of annual holiday. Overtime will not normally be included in the calculation of holiday pay, except where the overtime is contractually guaranteed.

In the event of termination of employment, you will be entitled to holiday pay calculated on a pro-rata basis in respect of all annual holiday already accrued but not taken at the date of termination of employment.

If, on termination of employment, you have taken more annual holiday entitlement than you have accrued in that holiday year, an appropriate deduction will be made from your final payment.

Public Holidays:

Full-time employees are entitled to ....public holidays each year and part-time, weekend employees' entitlement to public holidays is calculated on a pro-rata basis. Where the coffee shop closes on a public holiday and the employee has exhausted his or her pro rata public holiday entitlement, the employee will not be paid for this day. If the employee wishes to be paid for this day, he or she should take this time from his or her annual holiday entitlement, or arrange to work on an alternative day, at the sole discretion of the owner in accordance with the needs of the business.

Public holidays are in addition to annual holiday entitlement.

Where a recognized public holiday falls on a Saturday or a Sunday, alternative dates will not be substituted for these.

Sick Pay:

If you are absent from work because of sickness or injury you will be entitled to Statutory Sick Pay, provided you meet the qualifying conditions.

Absence Reporting:

You are required to notify the Company as soon as possible of your sickness absence and the reasons for it. You should do this personally at the earliest opportunity to the coffee shop owner, no later than 10 a.m. on the first day of your absence.

Notice:

Following successful completion of your probationary period, you are required to give two weeks' notice in writing to terminate your employment with the Company.

Following successful completion of your probationary period, you are entitled to receive the following written notice of termination of employment from the Company:

End of probationary period but less than two years' continuous service:	One week.
Two years' continuous service or longer:	One week for each complete year of service up to a maximum of 12 weeks after 12 years' service.

The Company may exclude these notice provisions in the event of dismissal for gross misconduct.

The Company reserves the right to make payment in lieu of notice.

Disciplinary and Dismissal Appeals:

If you are dissatisfied with any disciplinary or dismissal decision taken in respect of you, you have the right of appeal.

Grievance Procedure:

Your employer encourages all employees to settle grievances informally. If, however, you have a grievance relating to any aspect of your employment which you would like to be resolved formally, you must set out the grievance and the basis for it in writing and submit it to the coffee shop owner.

Post-Termination Grievance:

Should you wish to raise a grievance after your employment has ended, you should submit the grievance in writing to the coffee shop owner.

Dress and Appearance:

You are required to dress smartly during working hours and to wear any Company clothing which has been supplied to you. Should you turn up for work dressed inappropriately, the Company reserves the right to send you home.

UNIFORMS:

It is a condition of your employment that you wear a uniform at all times during your working hours.

The Company will supply you with the necessary uniform at the Company's expense. You are expected to take care of this and to maintain it in a reasonable condition.

You are required to return your uniform in reasonable condition upon termination of your employment.

Health and Safety:

You are required to gain an understanding of the Company's health and safety procedures, observe them, and ensure that safety equipment and clothing are always used. The Company's health and safety information is displayed on the Coffee Shop notice board.

Staff Discount:

The Coffee Shop operates a staff discount scheme which you are entitled to take advantage of. Full details of the scheme are available from the coffee shop manager.

Changes to Terms of Employment:

The Company reserves the right to make reasonable changes to any of your terms and conditions of employment and will notify you in writing of such changes at the earliest opportunity and, in any event, within one month of such changes taking effect.

Declaration:

I understand that during the course of my employment it will be necessary for the Company to maintain personnel records in relation to my employment. Any information held concerning my employment which is personal data and which is processed by the Company for these purposes shall be processed only in accordance with the Data Protection Act 1998.

Acknowledgement:

I acknowledge receipt of this Statement. I have been shown the Employee Handbook. I confirm that I have read the Statement and the Employee Handbook which set out the principal rules, policies and procedures relating to my employment and which together with my offer letter form my written contract of employment.

Signed by the employee ....

Date..

Signed for and on behalf of **ANOTHER COFFEE SHOP LTD**

....

Date..

APPENDIX 4
JOB DESCRIPTION PRO FORMA

Another Coffee Shop
125 Broccoli Street
Glasgow
G21 9AB

Post: Catering Assistant

Wage ....

Responsible to:

Job Purpose: Undertake duties connected with the preparation, simple cooking and service of food.

Main Duties: Preparation of food and beverages and serving and clearing tables.

General kitchen and coffee shop duties including washing up, serving and clearing tables.

Cleaning duties including the kitchen equipment, the kitchen and the sitting area of the coffee shop.

Duties may include some cash handling.

All duties must be carried out to comply with the Health and Safety at Work Act and Environmental Health Procedures.

Where appropriate training facilities may be provided.

General conditions:

Arrive at work at least 5 minutes before scheduled time to be ready to start your shift on time.

Employees will be provided with and required to wear a clean pressed uniform and protective clothing required for the position.

There is a no smoking policy in force.

Staff cannot make personal telephone calls from the coffee shop phone. All mobile phones must be switched off during working hours.

In the event that you are not well enough to come in to work you must telephone the owner or manager as soon as possible to allow time to get another member of staff to cover your shift.

I understand that failing to keep to any of these policies may result in disciplinary measures.

Employee's signature ....Date...................

APPENDIX 5
EMPLOYEE HANDBOOK

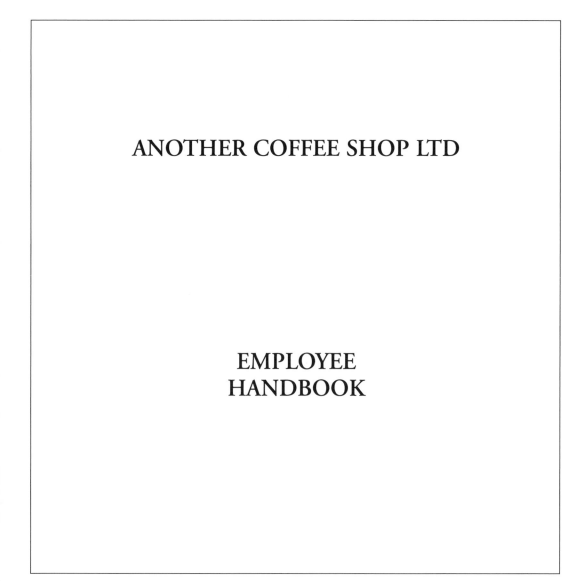

ANOTHER COFFEE SHOP LTD

EMPLOYEE
HANDBOOK

This is a copy of the handbook which I used in my coffee shop. It may appear somewhat excessive for some part-time coffee shop employees. However it is, I believe, prudent to cover as many of the 'bases' as possible.

My experience is that many a problem has been resolved before it had time to grow because of the existence of a detailed employee handbook.

CONTENTS

□ Holidays

□ Sick Pay Entitlement

□ Maternity Leave and Maternity Pay

□ Paternity Leave and Paternity Pay

□ Adoption Leave and Adoption Pay

□ Parental Leave

□ Time Off for Dependants

□ Disciplinary Procedure and Action

□ The Right to be Accompanied

□ Code of Conduct

□ Operational Policies and Procedures

□ Grievance Procedure

Holidays
ANNUAL HOLIDAYS

The holiday year runs from 1st January to 31st December. Employees' annual holiday entitlement in any holiday year is four weeks period, which part-time employees will receive on a pro rata basis.

Annual holiday entitlement accrues at the rate of one twelfth of the full annual holiday entitlement, on the 1st of each month, in advance.

Employees will be paid at their normal rate of pay and salaried employees will be paid their normal salary in respect of periods of annual holiday. Overtime will not normally be included in the calculation of holiday pay, except where the overtime is contractually guaranteed.

On termination of employment, employees will be entitled to holiday pay accrued but not taken at the date of termination of employment.

If, on termination of employment, an employee has taken more annual holiday than he or she has accrued in that holiday year, an appropriate deduction will be made from the employee's final pay.

PUBLIC HOLIDAYS

Full-time employees are entitled to .... public holidays each year:

Public holidays are in addition to annual holiday entitlement.

Sick Pay Entitlement
STATUTORY SICK PAY

Employees who are absent from work because of sickness will normally be entitled to receive Statutory Sick Pay (SSP) from the Company providing they meet the relevant criteria.

Once the criteria have been met, SSP is not normally payable for the first three days of sickness absence, unless the employee has been absent and in receipt of SSP within the previous eight weeks. Thereafter the Company will normally pay SSP at the statutory rate in force for a maximum of 28 weeks.

In order to qualify for SSP the employee must notify the Company on the first qualifying day, and submit a certificate of absence as soon as practicable. The Company reserves the right to withhold payment of SSP where an employee fails to follow the correct procedure. Certain employees are excluded from the SSP scheme, e.g. employees who earn below the lower earnings limit for National Insurance purposes.

Maternity Leave and Maternity Pay

Pregnant employees and employees who have recently given birth have a variety of rights under current legislation. This area of law is very complex, and the following sections provide only a general guide for employees.

INTRODUCTION

In general every employee who is pregnant has the right to Ordinary Maternity Leave of 26 weeks from day one of employment. In addition, women who have been continuously employed for 26 weeks at the beginning of the 15th week before the expected week of childbirth are entitled to a further 26 weeks Additional Maternity Leave, providing a total statutory entitlement of 52 weeks maternity leave.

It should also be noted that women are legally obliged to take a minimum of two weeks maternity leave after giving birth. This is called Compulsory Maternity Leave.

ORDINARY MATERNITY LEAVE

An employee who qualifies for the Ordinary Maternity Leave is entitled to receive all her normal contractual benefits (including annual holiday entitlement), excluding pay, while she is absent from work.

An employee is entitled to return to her original job at the end of the Ordinary Maternity Leave period.

ADDITIONAL MATERNITY LEAVE

An employee who qualifies for Additional Maternity Leave has the right to a further 26 weeks' leave, which will run directly from the end of her Ordinary Maternity Leave period. This additional leave is unpaid.

The employee's contract of employment continues throughout Additional Maternity Leave. The employee is entitled to return to her original job at the end of Additional Maternity Leave. However, if this is not reasonably practicable, she should be offered a similar job on no less favourable terms and conditions.

NOTIFICATION PROCEDURES FOR MATERNITY LEAVE

The notification requirements for maternity leave are exactly the same for Ordinary and Additional Maternity Leave. To qualify for maternity leave the employee must comply with the rules and procedures set out below.

□ A minimum of 15 weeks before the expected week of childbirth, the employee must give her employer notice of:

(a) the fact that she is pregnant;

(b) her expected week of childbirth, which must be confirmed with the medical certificate MATB1; and

(c) the date on which she intends to start her maternity leave. This must be in writing if requested by the employer.

☐ Within 28 days of the employee giving notice, the employer must respond in writing to the employee, confirming her full entitlement to maternity leave (both 26 weeks' Ordinary Maternity Leave and, if applicable, 26 weeks' Additional Maternity Leave) and the date when she is expected to return to work.

☐ The earliest the employee may start her maternity leave is 11 weeks before the expected week of childbirth. An employee may change her mind about when she wants to start her leave, providing she gives her employer at least 28 days' notice of the change.

☐ The employee does not need to give notice of her return to work if she simply returns at the end of her maternity leave period. However, if she wishes to return to work before her full entitlement to maternity leave has ended, she must give her employer a minimum of 28 days' notice of the date of her earlier return.

☐ If the employee fails to give the required 28 days' notice of an earlier return to work, the employer may postpone the employee's return until the end of the 28 days' notice she should have given, or until the end of her maternity leave period, whichever is earlier.

☐ An employee does not lose the right to return to work if she does not follow the correct notification requirements. However, her employer may take appropriate disciplinary action if she fails to return to work at the end of her maternity leave period.

STATUTORY MATERNITY PAY

All employees who have been continuously employed for at least 26 weeks ending with the 15th week before the expected week of childbirth (the Notification Week), and who satisfy the following conditions, are entitled to receive Statutory Maternity Pay (SMP) from their employer. The employee must:

☐ still be pregnant at the 11th week before her expected week of childbirth or have had the baby by that time;

☐ have average weekly earnings equal to or above the Lower Earnings Limit for National Insurance purposes over the eight-week period up to and including the Notification Week;

☐ give her employee a minimum of 28 days' notice that she intends to be absent from work because of her pregnancy;

☐ provide her employer with medical certification of her expected week of childbirth, normally using form MAT B1.

Statutory Maternity Pay is payable for up to 26 weeks. The first six weeks are payable at the higher rate which is 90% of the employee's normal earnings. The remaining 20 weeks are payable at a standard rate which changes from time to time. Where the employee's earnings are below the standard rate, the employee should be paid at 90% of her average earnings of the previous eight weeks up to and including the Notification Week.

ANTENATAL CARE

All pregnant employees are entitled to take time off with full pay during working hours to receive antenatal care. The employer may require an employee who wishes to take time off for these purposes to provide medical certification of her pregnancy and an appointment card, except in connection with the first appointment.

PREGNANCY-RELATED ABSENCE

An employee's maternity leave will automatically start if she is absent from work for a pregnancy-related absence during the four weeks before the baby is due.

Paternity Leave and Paternity Pay

Eligible employees (see below) are entitled to take up to two weeks' paid Paternity Leave following the birth of their child in order to care for the child or support its mother. During Paternity Leave, most employees will be entitled to Statutory Paternity Pay (SPP), which will be the same as the standard rate of Statutory Maternity Pay (SMP).

ELIGIBILITY FOR PATERNITY LEAVE AND PATERNITY PAY

In order to qualify for Paternity Leave and Statutory Paternity Pay the employee must:

☐ be the biological father of the child or the mother's husband or partner (male or female);

☐ have or expect to have responsibility for the child's upbringing;

☐ have worked continuously for the employer for 26 weeks leading into the Notification Week (the 15th week before the child is due); and

☐ have average weekly earnings equal to or above the Lower Earnings Limit for National Insurance purposes over the eight week period leading up to and including the Notification Week.

Employers may ask an employee to provide a self certificate as evidence that he or she meets these conditions. The self certificate must provide the information required above and include a declaration that the employee meets the necessary conditions.

TAKING PATERNITY LEAVE

An employee is permitted to take Paternity Leave in units of either one whole week or two consecutive whole weeks. Leave may start on any day of the week of or following the child's birth but must be completed:

☐ within 56 days of the actual date of birth of the child; or

☐ if the child is born early, within the period from the actual date of birth up to 56 days after the expected week of birth.

NOTIFICATION PROCEDURES FOR PATERNITY LEAVE

An employee who wishes to take Paternity Leave must notify the employer by the 15th week before the expected week of childbirth, stating:

☐ the week the child is due;

☐ whether the employee wishes to take one week or two weeks leave; and

☐ when the employee wants the leave to start.

CONTRACTUAL BENEFITS DURING PATERNITY LEAVE

An employee on Paternity Leave is entitled to benefit from normal terms and conditions of employment, with the exception of pay. The employee is entitled to return to the same job following Paternity Leave.

Adoption Leave and Adoption Pay

Employees who adopt a child may be entitled to adoption leave and Statutory Adoption Pay. This right applies to both men and women. There are special conditions relating to adoption leave and adoption pay. Employees who plan to adopt a child up to 18 years of age should discuss this with the employer, at which time their entitlements can be clarified.

Parental Leave

After one year's service, employees are entitled to a maximum of 13 weeks' unpaid Parental Leave for each of their children under five years old.

Parents of disabled children are entitled to a total of 18 weeks' parental leave, which can be taken at any point until the child's 18th birthday. Where an employee adopts a child under the age of 18, he or she is entitled to Parental Leave during the five years after the adoption, or until the child's 18th birthday, whichever is earlier. Employees who are entitled to parental leave should discuss their entitlements and conditions with the employer.

TIME OFF FOR DEPENDANTS

Employees are entitled to take reasonable unpaid time off to deal with sudden or unexpected problems with a dependant. A dependant is a partner, child or parent who lives with the employee as part of his or her family or any other person who reasonably relies on the employee for assistance.

Reasonable time off will be granted in appropriate circumstances.

The right is only to deal with emergencies and to put care arrangements in place. This means that in the case of a dependant's illness, for example, the employee is not entitled to time off for the duration of the dependant's illness.

Disciplinary Procedure and Action

The primary objective of the Company's Disciplinary Procedure is to ensure that all disciplinary matters are dealt with fairly and consistently.

For employees with 12 months' continuous service or longer, the Company will follow the Disciplinary Procedure set out below.

DISCIPLINARY PROCEDURE

Where appropriate all allegations of potential disciplinary offences will be investigated to establish the facts. A prior investigation may be judged as inappropriate only in very straightforward circumstances, e.g. lateness. The Company will give the employee the opportunity to state his or her case at a disciplinary meeting before taking any disciplinary action. The Company will give the employee reasonable notice of the requirement to attend a disciplinary meeting to allow the employee to prepare his or her case.

Following the disciplinary meeting, the Company may take disciplinary action against the employee. In any event, the employee will be informed of the outcome of the meeting as soon as possible.

Employees have the right to appeal against any disciplinary action taken against them in accordance with the Disciplinary and Dismissals Appeals Procedure.

DISCIPLINARY ACTION

The severity of the disciplinary action, if any, will be determined by the severity of the offence. For relatively minor first offences the Company will normally impose a Verbal Warning. If the employee persists with the offence in question, the Company may, having followed the Disciplinary Procedure in each instance, apply a Written Warning followed by Final Written Warning and eventually dismiss the employee.

For more severe first offences the Company may apply a Written Warning or Final Written Warning. In cases of gross misconduct the Company will normally dismiss the employee summarily, i.e. without notice.

A summary of the disciplinary actions that may be imposed is set out below.

Verbal Warning: The Company will advise the employee that his or her standard of conduct or performance has been unacceptable and that a failure to improve will result in further disciplinary action. The required standard will be outlined. The warning will be given verbally and subsequently confirmed in writing.

Written Warning: As for a Verbal Warning, but normally applied following a second disciplinary offence (but may be applied after a more serious first offence).

The employee will be advised in writing that a failure to improve the standard of conduct or performance will result in further disciplinary action.

Final Written Warning: As for a Written Warning, but normally applied following a third disciplinary offence. The employee will be advised in writing that a failure to improve the standard of conduct or performance will result in dismissal.

Dismissal: The employee is dismissed either with or without notice. Dismissal without notice is referred to as 'summary dismissal' and is normally restricted to cases of gross misconduct.

DISCIPLINARY APPEAL

The employee has the right to appeal against any disciplinary action against them.

THE RIGHT TO BE ACCOMPANIED

Employees are entitled to be accompanied at any formal disciplinary, grievance or appeal meeting. An employee under the age of 18 may choose to be accompanied by a parent or legal guardian.

Code of Conduct

COMPANY RULES

ATTENDANCE AND TIMEKEEPING

Employees are required to comply with the rules relating to notification of absence set out in the Company's Absence Policy and Procedure.

Employees are required to arrive at work promptly, ready to start work at their contracted starting times. Employees are required to remain at work until their contracted finishing times.

Employees must obtain authorization if for any reason they wish to arrive later or leave earlier than their agreed normal start and finish times.

The Company reserves the right not to pay employees in respect of working time lost because of poor timekeeping.

Persistent poor timekeeping will result in disciplinary action.

STANDARDS AND CONDUCT

Employees are required to maintain satisfactory standards of performance at work.

Employees are required to comply with all reasonable management instructions.

Employees are required to ensure the maintenance of acceptable standards of politeness.

Employees are required to take all necessary steps to safeguard the Company's public image and preserve positive relationships with its customers.

Employees are required to ensure that they behave in a way that does not constitute unlawful discrimination.

Personal mobile telephones must be switched off at all times during normal working hours.

FLEXIBILITY

Employees may be required to work additional hours at short notice, in accordance with the needs of the business. Employees may be required from time to time to undertake duties outside their normal job remit.

WORK CLOTHING

Where work clothing or uniforms are provided by the Company, they must be worn at all times during working hours. Employees are responsible for ensuring that all items of work clothing or uniform are kept clean and maintained in reasonable condition at all times and returned to the Company on termination of employment.

HEALTH AND SAFETY

Employees are required to gain an understanding of the Company's health and safety procedures, observe them, and ensure that safety equipment and clothing are always used. Employees must report all accidents, however small, as soon as possible, making an entry in the Company's Accident Book.

GROSS MISCONDUCT

Set out below are examples of behaviour which the Company treats as gross misconduct. Such behaviour may result in dismissal without notice. This list is not exhaustive.

- □ theft, dishonesty or fraud;

- □ smoking on the business premises;

- □ sleeping during working hours;

- □ assault, acts of violence or aggression;

- □ unacceptable use of obscene or abusive language;

- □ possession or use of, or being under the influence of, non-prescribed drugs or alcohol on the premises or during working hours;

- □ wilful damage to Company, employee or customer property;

- □ serious insubordination;

- □ serious or gross negligence;

- □ unlawful discrimination, including acts of indecency or sexual harassment;

- □ refusal to carry out reasonable management instructions;

- □ serious breach of the Health and Safety policies and procedures.

Operational Policies and Procedures

Harassment

Harassment is physical, verbal or non-verbal behaviour which is unwanted and personally offensive to the recipient, and which causes the recipient to feel threatened, humiliated, intimidated, patronized, denigrated, bullied, distressed or harassed.

If an employee is accused of unlawful discrimination or harassment, the Company will investigate the matter fully. Any breach of this rule will be treated as gross misconduct and is likely to result in summary dismissal.

ABSENCE PROCEDURE AND RULES

Employees must ensure that any time off (other than in the case of sickness) is authorized in advance by their manager. Employees should complete an Absence Form on their first day back at work.

Medical and Dental Appointments

Employees are requested to arrange any medical or dental appointments outside working hours. Where this is not possible, employees must obtain permission from management before taking any time off and appointments should be arranged for first thing in the morning or last thing at night to minimize any disruptions to the Company.

Absence Due to Sickness

Employees are required to notify the Company as soon as possible of their sickness absence and the reasons for it. They should do this personally at the earliest opportunity to their line manager, no later than the time their shift starts, on the first day of the absence.

It is essential that employees keep the Company updated on the circumstances of the absence and of its estimated duration.

Where an employee's absence lasts more than seven calendar days a Medical Certificate completed by a medical practitioner must be given to the coffee shop owner.

ALCOHOL AND DRUGS

Consumption of Alcohol on the Premises

Employees are expressly forbidden to consume alcohol when at work or to bring it onto Company premises. Any breach of this rule will be treated as gross misconduct and is likely to result in summary dismissal.

Drug Misuse or Abuse on the Premises

Employees who take, sell or buy non-prescription drugs during working hours or on Company premises will be committing an act of gross misconduct and are likely to be summarily dismissed.

Intoxication at Work

An employee who is under the influence of alcohol or drugs during working hours or on Company premises will be escorted from the premises immediately. The Company will take disciplinary action when the employee has had time to sober up or recover from the effects of drugs. Intoxication at work will normally be treated as gross misconduct and result in summary dismissal.

DRESS AND APPEARANCE GUIDELINES

If a uniform or specified clothing is not provided, employees are required to dress in a manner appropriate to the function in which they are engaged.

All employees are required to attend work each day either in the supplied uniform or in normal smart dress suitable for a working environment which involves regular contact with customers, and to maintain high standards of personal hygiene.

All employees must ensure their clothing is clean, ironed and in good condition, free from rips and tears. Footwear should normally be dark, kept clean and in good condition.

Employees should not wear fingernail varnish, should keep their hair tidy and must ensure that their hands and nails are clean when at work.

UNIFORMS AND COMPANY CLOTHING

It is a condition of employment that employees wear any uniforms or clothing specified by the Company at all times during working hours.

The Company will supply employees with the appropriate uniforms or clothing at the Company's expense. Employees are expected to take care of any such items and to maintain them in a reasonable condition.

Employees must return any uniforms or clothing supplied by the Company at the termination of their employment. The Company reserves the right to deduct from the employee's final pay the cost of any uniforms or clothing that are lost, damaged or not returned.

CASH HANDLING

Only those employees specifically authorized by the Company to do so may have access to or use cash tills. Employees who use or attempt to use cash tills without being so authorized will be subject to disciplinary action.

Employees are not permitted to give discounts on any food or drink without permission of the manager.

FOOD HANDLING AND HYGIENE

Employees must always wash their hands before handling food and particularly after using the toilet.

Employees must inform the owner at once of any skin, nose, throat or bowel conditions.

Employees must inform the owner if anyone at home, or any pet or animal with which they have contact, is suffering from diarrhoea or vomiting.

Employees must ensure that any cuts or sores they may have are covered with a coloured (not skin-tinted) waterproof dressing.

Employees must ensure that protective clothing is clean and worn at all times.

Employees are not permitted to smoke during food preparation or in serving areas during working hours.

Employees should be careful not to cough and sneeze over or near food.

Employees should ensure that all equipment and surfaces are scrupulously clean at all times.

Employees should take care to keep the handling of food to a minimum and should not let their hands touch their clothes, face, nose, mouth or hair while handling food.

Employees must ensure that unused food is disposed of properly.

Employees must ensure that they wash their hands after handling bins and rubbish.

TRAINING

Whenever a new employee joins the Company, it is the employer's duty to ensure that he or she is given a proper introduction to the workplace, colleagues, environmental health and health and safety procedures.

Within the first few days of employment the new employee's training requirements will be assessed and arrangements made for that training to be provided. Training will be met by a combination of 'on the job' and related 'in house' training. From time to time, however, it may be necessary to arrange external training.

Each induction process will be tailored to the individual employee.

REDUNDANCY, SHORT-TIME WORKING AND LAY-OFF

It is the Company's intention to develop its business and to provide security of employment for its employees. However, circumstances may arise when changes in the market will lead to the need for reductions in employees.

Where a redundancy situation arises, the Company will give consideration to alternative options.

Selection for redundancy will be based on criteria drawn up at the time, and will be assessed in an objective manner.

APPENDIX 6
CUSTOMER QUESTIONNAIRE

To help us improve our service and food it would be very helpful if you could answer the following questions and leave your comments and suggestions. Please post the questionnaire into the box on the counter when you have completed it.

POLITENESS AND FRIENDLINESS OF STAFF
☐ Could be improved ☐ Good ☐ Very Good ☐ Excellent

SPEED OF SERVICE
☐ Could be improved ☐ Good ☐ Very Good ☐ Excellent

CHOICE OF FOOD
☐ Could be improved ☐ Good ☐ Very Good ☐ Excellent

CHOICE OF DRINKS
☐ Could be improved ☐ Good ☐ Very Good ☐ Excellent

PRESENTATION OF FOOD
☐ Could be improved ☐ Good ☐ Very Good ☐ Excellent

TASTE OF FOOD (Please say what you had to eat.)
☐ Could be improved ☐ Good ☐ Very Good ☐ Excellent

VALUE FOR MONEY
☐ Could be improved ☐ Good ☐ Very Good ☐ Excellent

GENERAL CLEANLINESS
☐ Could be improved ☐ Good ☐ Very Good ☐ Excellent

Would you come back to the coffee shop?   Yes   ....

                                                     Perhaps ....

                                                     No   ....

Please give your comments and suggestions in the space below.

Name ....

Address ....

....

....

Telephone number ....

APPENDIX 7
USEFUL CONTACT NUMBERS
AND ADDRESSES

The following is an index of useful contact addresses, most of which have been referred to in the text of the book.

Alexandra – www.alexandra.co.uk – 08700 600 200
For aprons, uniforms, white coats and chefs' jackets

Baco – www.baco.co.uk – 01236 733 954 and 0191 378 0088
For all baking ingredients and cake and scone mixes

British Franchising Association – www.british-franchise.org.uk – 01491 578050

Business Debtline – 0800 197 6026

Business Start-ups

> England – Business Link: 0845 6009006 – www.businesslink.gov.uk

> Wales – Business Eye: 0845 7969798 – www.businesseye.org.uk

> Scotland – Small Business Gateway: 0845 6096611– www.b.gateway.co.uk

> Northern Ireland – 02890 239090 www.nibusinessinfo.co.uk

> Highlands and Islands Enterprise – www.hie.co.uk

Cobweb Information Ltd – factsheet on dismissing staff – www.scavenger.net

Coffee Beans and Coffee Machines – www.matthewalgie.co.uk – 0141 429 2817

Companies House – www.companies-house.gov.uk – 0870 333 3636

Department of Trade and Industry – advice on resolving disputes
www.dti.gov.uk/er/resolvingdisputes.htm

Equal Opportunities Commission – www.eoc.org.uk – 0845 601 5901

Food Safety Management Packs

These packs are available from the FSA.

> **England**: it is known as 'Safer Food, Better Business'. You can contact 0845 606 0667 for a copy or you can view it online at www.food.gov.uk/sfbb

> **Scotland**: it is known as 'Cook Safe' and you can contact 0845 606 0667 for a copy or you can view it online at www.food.gov.uk or you can contact your local authority for more information.

> **Northern Ireland** has produced a guidance pack known as 'Safe Catering' and you should contact your local authority for more information.

> **Wales**: some Welsh authorities are using 'Safer Food, Better Business' which you can view online at www.food.gov.uk/sfbb or contact your local authority for more information.

Food Standards Agency for publications – 0845 606 0667; email foodstandards @ecgroup.uk.com, www.food.gov.uk

Food Standards Agency for caterers – www.food.gov.uk/cleanup

Franchise Direct – www.franchisedirect.co.uk
If you are thinking of taking on a franchise

Health and Safety Executive – www.hse.gov.uk – 08701 545500
Information Line – 08701 545 500
Book ordering line – 0178 788 1165

Home Office – www.homeoffice.gov.uk – 0845 010 6677
If you are considering employing overseas staff

HM Revenue and Customs – www.hmrc.gov.uk
Working for yourself – The Guide – to order – 0845 9000 404

Inland Revenue – www.inlandrevenue.gov.uk

Job Centre Plus – www.jobcentreplus.gov.uk

Law Society – See local telephone directory for your nearest Law Society

Microfibre cloths – www.micro-pro.co.uk
For information on microfibre cloths for use in the kitchen

National Minimum Wage helpline – 0845 600 0678

New employers' helpline – 0845 607 8787

Nisbets Catering Equipment and work wear – www.nisbets.com – 0845 140 5555

Part-time workers' regulations – www.dti.gov.uk/er/ptime.htm

Paul Wigley breakthrough facilitator – www.howmightwe.co.uk
email paul@howmightwe.co.uk – 0777 805 8026

Performing Rights Society – www.prs.co.uk – 0207 580 5544

Rich Sauces – 02891 819004
For luxury mayonnaise and different-flavoured mayonnaise

Royal Institute of British Architects – www.architecture.com

Royal Institute of Chartered Surveyors – www.ric.org

Supplier of Scottish Smoked Salmon, smoked duck etc. – 01292 442 773;
email hello@burnsmoke.com

VAT registration – 0845 010 9000

XS Stock Ltd – www.xs-stock.com – 01294 204 004
For microfibre cloths etc.

INDEX

Other related titles from How To Books

MARKETING FOR THE MICRO-BUSINESS

Companies owned by individuals and partners have the challenge of finding enough profitable customers for the business to generate a living for the owners. Although passionate about what they do, passion alone is rarely enough. Marketing is often the answer, but only if done effectively. This book shows sole-traders and small businesses with up to 20 employees how to use marketing effectively. If you've ever wondered how to spend your limited budget to find more customers, this book will give you the answers you need. If you don't know where to advertise or how to produce an effective advert, this book will tell you.

ISBN 978-1-84528-286-8

PREPARING A WINNING BUSINESS PLAN

'This book will not only help you prepare a business plan but will also provide a basic understanding of how to start up a business.' – *Working from Home*

'An excellent reference for even the most inexperienced business person looking to march into the business world ably armed with a professional plan.' – *Home Business Alliance*

ISBN 978-1-84528-302-5

BOOK-KEEPING & ACCOUNTING
FOR THE SMALL BUSINESS

'...compulsory reading for those starting a new business and for those already in the early stages.' – *Manager, National Westminster Bank (Midlands)*

'An easy-to-understand manual on double-entry book-keeping that anyone can follow.' – *Business First*

ISBN 978-1-85703-878-1

THE SMALL BUSINESS START-UP WORKBOOK

'I would urge every business adviser in the land to read this book'
– *Sylvia Tidy-Harris, Managing Director of www.womenspeakers.co.uk*

'Inspirational and practical workbook that takes you from having a business idea to actually having a business. By the time you have worked through the exercises and checklists you will be focussed, confident and raring to go.' – *www.allthatwomenwant.co.uk*

'A real 'must have' for anyone thinking of setting up their own venture.'
– *Thames Valley News*

'… a very comprehensive book, a very readable book.' – *Sister Business E-Zine*

ISBN 978-1-84528-038-3

SETTING UP & RUNNING A LIMITED COMPANY
ROBERT BROWNING

'Many businesses are run through companies but there are legal implications, and careful consideration is required before forming a limited company. This guide sets out the pros and cons, and how to proceed.' – *Landlordzone.co.uk*

ISBN 978-1-85703-866-8

85 INSPIRING WAYS TO MARKET YOUR SMALL BUSINESS
JACKIE JARVIS

This book is for the many people who run their own small to medium sized business and who want to make it grow. It sets out some great ideas and explains how each idea will benefit your business, what you need to do to make it work, and how you can apply it to your own business *immediately*.

ISBN 978-1-84528-167-0

Other Small Business Start-up titles from How To Books

HOW TO START AND RUN A PETSITTING BUSINESS

This book guides you, step by step, through the process of setting up your own petsitting business with information on everything from researching the market, naming your business, legal issues, animal law, pet care, advertising, interviewing your first client – and their owners! – to sample petsitting contracts, insurance, licensing and other issues fundamental to petsitting in the twenty first century.

Packed full of vital advice, invaluable tips and accounts of the author's and other petsitters' experiences – both heart-warming and educational, this book is a must have for any pet loving entrepreneur.

ISBN 978-1-84528-289-9

STARTING & RUNNING A SUCCESSFUL CLEANING BUSINESS

The cleaning industry is worth billions each year. There is plenty of money to be made and you don't require any specific qualifications to get started. What you do need is a range of key personal skills as well as a determination to succeed. This book will provide you with an invaluable insight into the world of office and domestic cleaning. It will enable you to start, build and run your own successful cleaning company.

ISBN 978-1-84528-284-4

STARTING & RUNNING A GREETINGS CARD BUSINESS

Making and selling greetings cards is one of the most popular ways for creative people to set up in business. It is also popular as a part-time business that can be run from home and started with a limited amount of capital. This book takes you step by step through the process of starting and running a business with lots of useful practical advice to help you.

ISBN 978-1-84528-264-6

RUNNING A BED AND BREAKFAST: A LANDLADY'S GUIDE

Running a small B&B in your home can be an interesting and fulfilling job as well as being one that will enable you to work from home because of family or other commitments. It's also a good way of earning money from those empty bedrooms once your children have fled the nest. If you are widowed or retired, running a B&B will supplement your income. In this book Christabel Milner, who has run a series of small Bed and Breakfast businesses by herself, explores the issues and shows you how to make a success of it. She covers all subjects from choosing the bed linen to safeguarding your own personal security.

ISBN 978-1-84528-269-1

How To Books

are available through all good bookshops,
or you can order direct from us through Grantham Book Services.

Tel: +44 (0)1476 541080
Fax: +44 (0)1476 541061
Email: orders@gbs.tbs-ltd.co.uk

Or via our website
www.howtobooks.co.uk

To order via any of these methods
please quote the title(s) of the book(s)
and your credit card number together with its expiry date.

For further information about our books and catalogue,
please contact:

How To Books
Spring Hill House
Spring Hill Road
Begbroke
Oxford
OX5 1RX

Visit our web site at
www.howtobooks.co.uk

Or you can contact us by email at
info@howtobooks.co.uk